Ruth Nelson

BARBARA J. BOLTON

ways to help them learn

children · grades 1 to 6

G/L REGAL BOOKS

INTERNATIONAL CENTER FOR LEARNING

A Division of G/L Publications, Glendale, California, U.S.A.

Published by Regal Books Division, G/L Publications. Glendale, California 91209, U.S.A.

Library of Congress Catalog Card No. 77-168843. ISBN 0-8307-0119-2.

Photos by Douglas Gilbert.

CONTENTS

Preface

PART I: SEE HOW THEY GROW

PART II: SEE HOW THEY LEARN

PART III: SEE THEM IN ACTION

Bibliography

Training materials for use with this handbook
are available from your church supplier.

THE AUTHOR

Barbara J. Bolton earned a B.A. degree at Whittier College and an M.A. degree in elementary education at California State College, Los Angeles.

Her teaching career spans kindergarten through sixth grade over the past 20 years. She is a specialist in the field of remedial reading.

Barbara is active in the Christian Church, and has held nearly every office in her Sunday school, including a two-year term as Christian Education Director. She has worked with Sunday school children and teachers from kindergarten through the sixth grade levels. Her writing experience includes articles for TEACH magazine, and Junior Sunday school curriculum materials.

The late Dr. Henrietta C. Mears, founder of Gospel Light Publications and distinguished Christian education leader for more than 40 years, often said, "Good teachers are not born; they are made by conscientious labor." It is axiomatic that if one is to be successful in any field, he must be trained. Our Lord recognized this fact in training the Twelve. First He spent the whole night in prayer in preparation for the momentous task of choosing them. From this point the teaching and training of these men became a matter of paramount importance to Him.

A tremendous passion for the training of leadership has been a hallmark in the program of Gospel Light. What workers learn today will determine what the church will be tomorrow. This is the great need of the hour: To train leaders for Christian service, particularly for the Sunday school, who will know how to administer and teach. With a deep sense of obligation as well as opportunity the International Center for Learning was created in 1970 to specialize in the training of dedicated personnel in all departments of the local church.

This is one of a series of textbooks designed to train workers in the Sunday school. It has grown out of actual proven experience and represents the best in educational philosophy. In addition to textual materials, the full program of ICL includes audiovisual media and church leadership training seminars sponsored in strategic centers across America and ultimately overseas as rapidly as God enables. We are being deluged with requests to help in the momentous task of training workers. We dare not stop short of providing all possible assistance.

Train for Sunday school success! Train for church growth! Train people by example and experience to pray and plan and perform. Christ trained the Twelve. Dare we do less?

Cyrus N. Nelson

President
Gospel Light Publications

PREFACE

To influence a child's life for eternity—what a wonderful opportunity for the church! Guiding the growth and development of children in their tender years should be a vital challenge for every Christian worker.

As we think about these opportunities and the responsibilities that accompany them, it is essential for us to become better acquainted with children, both as individuals and as group members. Let's begin by considering Jesus' relationships with children.

HE WAS INTERESTED IN CHILDREN

Jesus was concerned for and interested in the welfare of children. He was anxious to become a part of the lives of the children who were brought to Him. "Let the children come to Me, for the Kingdom of God belongs to such as they," were His words in Mark 10:14 *(TLB)*. He took them in His arms and blessed them (Mark 10:16).

HE MINISTERED TO THEIR PHYSICAL NEEDS

Jesus included children in His healing ministry. Take time now to read how Jesus healed Jairus' daughter (Mark 5:22-42), the nobleman's son (John 4:46-54), and the epileptic boy (Luke 9:37-43). He cared deeply for children who suffered and took time to minister to their needs.

HE RESPECTED THEM AS CHILDREN

Jesus revealed His respect for children when He said, "Beware that you don't look down upon a single one of these little children. For I tell you that in heaven their angels have constant access to My Father" (Matthew 18:10). He accepted them just as they were.

He stressed how highly He valued childhood in His words, "Any of you who welcomes a little child like this because you are Mine, is welcoming Me and caring for Me" (Matthew 18:5). In our relationships with children, we should give heed to His directions: "If someone causes one of these little ones who believes in Me to lose his faith—it would be better for that man if a huge millstone were tied around his neck and he were thrown into the sea" (Mark 9:42).

HE IS OUR EXAMPLE

As we prepare to plan meaningful learning experiences for children, we can look to Jesus for an example of teaching that will bring about effective learning. We will need to show the same loving concern and respect for each child with whom we come in contact. The importance of providing learning experiences which will meet the individual needs of each child cannot be overemphasized. Just as Jesus met the immediate needs of both children and adults, so we too must develop the flexibility which will permit us to deal with each child in the situation in which we find him. We must do this in such a way that he will know the love and concern of Jesus through us.

PART I

SEE HOW THEY GROW

1ST & 2ND GRADERS: WIDE-EYED WONDERERS

OBJECTIVE—*to know and understand the physical, emotional, social, intellectual, and spiritual needs and characteristics of sixes and sevens.*

When you move into the world of a six or seven year old child, be prepared for excitement and activity! The six year old is a busy, active, curious bundle of energy that is reaching out into the ever-widening world of new people, places and experiences. He is jumping over the boundaries of home and family to find his place in a world of friends, school and neighborhood. It often seems that he is going in many directions at the same time, with so many things to do and so many people to meet, that his hurrying and scurrying leave adults breathless.

For the seven year old, we see something of a slowing down that permits him to pull together the experiences of his brief past into a meaningful background upon which new relationships can be built.

PHYSICAL GROWTH

Both sixes and sevens are growing rapidly. Often we think only of children growing older and taller. At least five areas of growth are evident. All children grow five ways, but at different rates of speed. We can easily see the physical growth of children. It is a bit more difficult to measure spiritual, emotional, social and intellectual growth. However, learning experiences need to involve

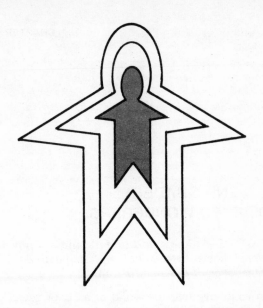

the total child if we are to avoid fragmented learning. If we are to insure the most effective learning possible, we must be aware of all areas of growth, and plan for needs in each area to be met.

The child of six or seven is going through a period of decreased physical growth. Coordination and muscle control are developing. The term "constant motion" may be used to describe the behavior of sixes and sevens. We should not be surprised to observe wriggling and squirming. His need to be a "doer" is ever present. Awareness of these physical characteristics will prompt us to plan appropriate activities.

EMOTIONAL GROWTH

Emotionally, the six year old is experimenting with new and frequently intense feelings. He is often unable to control behavior. He is bound to his home, but at the same time is adventuring out into a strange and sometimes confusing world. Making decisions is difficult. He is seeking independence but often must be very dependent. However, the six year old's behavior is usually eager, enthusiastic and filled with the enjoyment of life as he feels it.

The seven year old sometimes appears to withdraw within himself. He is very thoughtful and seems to absorb much more than he gives out. He is concerned about receiving adult approval in addition to approval of his peers. Our seven year old is beginning to set standards of achievement for himself.

Many conflicts are present in the life of the seven year old. He would like to become increasingly independent, but lacks self-confidence. He is often unable to accept the responsibility for his own actions. It is a confusing year of adjustment to his peer group and to adults.

INTELLECTUAL GROWTH

An intense eagerness to learn is a delightful and extremely important characteristic of the six year old. He asks innumerable questions and frequently tries to answer them through experimentation and discovery. Even though his attention span is short, he enjoys repetition. Familiar stories and activities can be very meaningful. A limited concept of time and space makes sixes think in terms of here and now, rather than of the past or future. Their listening and speaking vocabulary is well developed. As reading skill increases, the child begins to see the relationship between the spoken and written word. It is so important that we plan to encourage the eagerness that is present at this point in the child's life.

The attention span of the seven year old increases and his capabilities keep pace with his interest and enthusiasm. He is a good listener, but at the same time, can read with some degree of independence. He needs to have an opportunity to understand and to solve problems related to the here and now. However, he is beginning to do some abstract thinking, too. We need to provide some guidance in the selection of activities. Very often his desire for perfection will lead to a disappointing situation if the projected activity proves too difficult for him.

SOCIAL GROWTH

Sixes and sevens are struggling to become socially

acceptable in their peer groups. The concept of "Do for others what you want them to do for you"[1] is a difficult one for a six year old to accept. He feels that being first and winning are very important. Taking turns is a most difficult idea that needs to be practiced at every opportunity. Accepting the opinions and wishes of others enables the individual child to think about the welfare of the total group, as well as his own.

The seven year old is very concerned about making friends. He wants to please adults. He is also developing the needed skills to plan and work in group situations. There is still some difficulty in accepting group decisions if they differ from his own.

Both six and seven year olds need the warm, supportive, understanding friendship of adults in order to find their places in group situations. The child needs to value himself as a person and then to value each individual within the part of the world he knows. A child's social growth process involves a movement from "I" to "you" to "we."

SPIRITUAL GROWTH

Our deep concern for the spiritual growth of sixes and sevens leads us to explore their understandings and feelings about God, Jesus, the Bible and the Church, which they may have at this point in their development.

They are able to accept the fact of God as Creator, all-knowing and ever present, yet they ask many questions about the why and how of creation. They understand that God sent His Son, Jesus, as an expression of His great love. They begin to understand how Jesus can change lives. As they become better acquainted with the Bible, their understanding of God is enlarged. Sixes and sevens begin to use the Bible independently, as reading skills increase. They are able to grasp more and more the greatness of God's love as revealed in Bible stories.

This is a time when we should endeavor to help children develop a feeling for communication with God through prayer. Prayer needs to become a natural expression of gratitude or petition. We need to be careful to help each child understand that God, in His wisdom, will decide upon the appropriate answer to his prayers. He needs to grasp the concept that he can talk to God anywhere, any time, and in his own words. Then he will begin to feel the importance of prayer in his daily life.

If the child's experiences in church-related activities are happy, pleasant ones, he will think of the church as a happy place with loving, caring adults and children. He will think of it as a place where people learn of God. He will begin to understand some of the parts of the worship service and their significance to him as an individual.

In addition to knowing about God, Jesus, the Bible and the Church, it is of the utmost importance that sixes and sevens begin to develop strong values that will build a foundation for the years to come. Understanding and feeling, as important as they may be, are only stepping-stones to the application response in the daily lives of children. Workers in this department are a very important link in helping to transfer a child's feelings of love for God into visible responses. We need to find ways to show God's love to others. It will not be enough to talk about it.

A feeling of reverence can also become a part of the child's life. An appreciation for the Bible as an instrument to help us know God and to be able to obey and to trust Him is developed during these childhood years.

Relationships with other children and adults are influenced by the child's understandings and feelings about God, Jesus, the Bible and the Church. Kindness, fair play, thoughtfulness, love, obedience, concern for others, helpfulness, and forgiveness are but a few of the behavioral goals which may be developed as the child grows spiritually. In Ephesians 4:31,32, we read, "Stop being mean, bad-tempered and angry. Quarreling, harsh words, and dislike of others should have no place in your lives. Instead, be kind to each other, tender-hearted, forgiving one another, just as God has forgiven you because you belong to Christ."[2]

As adults who guide the learning experiences of children, we need to be concerned for the rights of the children with whom we work. Every child has the right to expect sincere love from the adults of his world. He needs to experience understanding and acceptance. Cooperation, involvement and discovery through learning activities are all essential factors. Feelings of success and acceptance are basic ingredients in our teaching programs if we are to be sure that each child is helped to develop to his greatest potential.

PUTTING KNOWLEDGE INTO ACTION

Considering the things we know about the characteristics and needs of children, how can we plan for a meaningful teaching program? We are concerned with guiding the total child. We will need to use many teaching methods. A variety of experiences which involve planning, exploring, discovering, evaluating, making choices, and questioning needs to be made available to children. Continuous planning and evaluation are necessary if we are to make desirable changes in our program that will result in a more effective teaching program.

CHECK TASK—*Assemble a "children's profile" loose leaf notebook. Include snapshots, magazine pictures, drawings, or sketches which will help to illustrate the growth pattern of the sixes and sevens in the five areas which were discussed. You may wish to include descriptive phrases.*

CHAPTER TWO

3RD & 4TH GRADERS: EXCITING EXPLORERS

OBJECTIVE—*to know and understand the physical, emotional, social, intellectual, and spiritual needs and characteristics of eights and nines.*

Think for a moment about a child you know that is eight or nine years old. What do you know about him? List words that describe his physical appearance. Compile a list of his interests. What are some leisure time activities he enjoys? What kinds of environments and experiences produce a positive reaction? What things in his surroundings cause a negative reaction? How does this child feel about himself? How does he relate to other children and to adults? Are you finding it difficult to answer these questions about a specific child? If so, keep him in mind as you continue to read this chapter.

PHYSICAL GROWTH

Physically, the eight and nine year old is in a period of steady growth. Coordination is well enough developed to allow him to react with speed and accuracy. These years are filled with rough and tumble activity. Development of the muscular system permits longer attention span. Eights and nines will work diligently and for increased periods of time on projects which are of interest to them. They enjoy adequate energy, much enthusiasm and enough self-confidence to permit them to be active participants in projects which capture their keen interest. Sometimes impatience at delay or inability to quickly accomplish desired goals is a noticeable characteristic.

EMOTIONAL GROWTH

The emotional growth and development of the eight and nine year old often surpasses his physical growth. Eights and nines are eager to explore the world around them. They are curious and frequently experiment beyond their capabilities.

The eight year old is torn between his need to be a child and his desire to be grown up. He is able to evaluate feelings with his peer group, but finds it more difficult to accept evaluative criticism from adults. Our eight year old is reaching out to others and becoming more concerned for other people than for himself. He is beginning to develop a sense of fair play and to be concerned with a value system that distinguishes between right and wrong.

As the eight year old becomes nine, he is able to be more independent in making choices. He becomes increasingly aware of the larger world about him and is concerned with the rights and feelings of others as his experiences extend beyond his family to his neighborhood and community. He may even express a strong interest in and curiosity about faraway places in the world. This is an excellent opportunity for involvement in the missionary program of the church.

SOCIAL GROWTH

Socially, the eight year old is experimenting with his peer group. It is important for him to belong. As his desire to have status within his peer group becomes more intense, his dependence upon adults decreases. At this time, the loving, understanding guidance of adults can be supportive as the child discovers that disagreements and problems occur with his peers in self-directed group activities.

Even though the eight year old is working for group approval, it seems to be important that he have a special friend and also a special enemy. These two special relationships usually develop with children of the same sex. Activities and interests are also usually dependent upon the same sex at this age.

Through the process of working, playing, and living with the peer group, the individual child begins to understand himself. He begins to accept his own limitations and skills. Self-respect is beginning to develop at this age. Feelings of fair play, consideration, mutual acceptance, understanding, cooperation and respect for others all begin to be an important part of the development of each child. These are all characteristics which we hope to instill and strengthen in our eight year olds so they will become an integral part of the emerging adult. What a critical time for Sunday school teachers!

Usually nine year olds are able to criticize themselves. Even though self-respect is developed to permit failure, it is important that adult guidance still be present. The nine year old would like to be independent enough to make his own decisions, but subtle adult guidance is often needed. He responds well to adult concern and interest.

Group influence continues to be strong in the life of the nine year old. He is more able to plan and work through an activity with success than he was at eight. A cooperative activity can be planned and carried through with real enthusiasm and success. This is an ideal time to include church-related group activities or clubs into the total plan of the church.

INTELLECTUAL GROWTH

Let's consider the intellectual growth and development of eight and nine year olds. Communication skills of the eight year old are developing at a rapid rate. Individual differences among children can result in rapid progress for some readers and limited progress for others. Both eight and nine year olds are interested in using their newly developed reading skills to read portions of the Bible. They want to know more about Bible characters. They question adults constantly. The ability to talk surpasses the ability to read in many children of eight.

Learning games interest the eight year old. He is able to take turns in a small group. His interest span widens as he is exposed to more experiences. His concepts of time, space and distance are increasing. He is able to relate to the past and to the future, as well as to the present.

Creativity is at a peak in the eight year old. Creative art and drama both provide activities which will develop into valuable learning experiences. The expression of thoughts and feelings through art and drama help the eight year old work through problem situations. They can help him internalize Bible information which will encourage him to exhibit Christian behavior. The application of God's Word to daily living can often be brought about by creative drama.

At nine years, the child begins to become a reasoning person. He realizes that there may be more than one answer to a question, more than one idea about a given subject, and more than one opinion which may be expressed in a discussion. He is willing to listen to ideas presented by adults, as well as those from his peer group. He enjoys looking up information and discovering his own answers to problems and questions.

The nine year old is searching for self-identity. Think of the marvelous opportunity presented to the Sunday school worker! He can provide a Christian model at a time when the child is most eagerly searching for one.

The nine year old does not usually have difficulty

understanding and accepting the teachings of the church. He is concerned about discovering the truth. He is anxious to develop a code of right and wrong. This code, however, must be flexible enough to allow him further exploration and discovery in his search for a positive self-concept.

SPIRITUAL GROWTH

Eight and nine year olds enjoy attending Sunday school and church. They need to feel that God loves them. They need to have an opportunity to be surrounded by church activities that are meaningful to them, a Christian home, and a Christian influence in the community.

Learning to make choices and decisions based upon feelings of right and wrong is also important at this time in the child's life. Sometimes it is difficult for him to admit wrongdoing. We can encourage him to act with Christian motivation, and help him understand the loving, forgiving nature of God. We can also help him satisfy his need to forgive others.

The prayer life of the eight and nine year old is filled with honesty, simplicity and trust. It is important for him to realize that God stands ready to help and that He will hear his prayer at any time. We need to assist him in developing an understanding and assurance of God's love and answer to prayer. It is sometimes difficult for children of this age to know that God's answer to prayer is best, even though it is not always answered in just the way they might want it to be. Understanding that God is an all-wise, all-knowing, all-powerful and loving God begins to become a part of the child's beliefs and feelings. Knowing that God loves and cares for him as an important and valued individual helps to increase the child's acceptance of himself.

Eights and nines need to understand what it means to need Jesus as their personal Saviour. Children who indicate an awareness of sin and a concern about accepting Jesus as Saviour need to be carefully guided without pressure. Opportunities to experience trust, love, sorrow, wrongdoing, and forgiveness in his daily life will help the child to understand and accept the love and forgiveness of God.

THE SITUATION FOR GROWTH

In a world that exerts day-by-day pressure for improvement and development, the church can provide this growth through a number of factors. These should include love, careful guidance, security, acceptance, exposure to beauty, and opportunities for maturity and worship. This type of environment will help contribute to the development of a positive self-concept. Every child has a right to feel that he is an important person not only to God, but to the people with whom he comes in contact. It is the responsibility of the Sunday school worker to know each child as a person. A concern about his well-being is essential. It is not enough to know the child on Sunday morning. The Sunday school worker must plan to know each child at home, at school, and in his neighborhood. Involvement with the total child is a necessity if he is to have the opportunity to grow and develop to his potential.

When the Sunday school teacher chooses methods and activities for his pupils, he must consider the skills which they possess at each stage in their lives. Our eights and nines are enthusiastic about using reading and research skills. Their increased manual skills and interest in drama and art activities offer many opportunities for meaningful experiences.

PUT YOUR INSIGHTS TO WORK!

Take a few moments now to pull together the information you have about the eight or nine year old. Once again, think about the child that you know. On the basis of your information about him, follow these suggestions:

List his physical characteristics.

Discover his interests.

Make a list of his needs. Remember that they may be needs typical of this age group or they may be needs important only to this individual child.

What are his skills and strengths?

If you have all of this information available to you, it will be possible for you to plan a Sunday school program which will meet the needs of the child. Now, thinking about all of these factors, determine a variety of methods which may be used by the Sunday school to provide effective learning experiences for this child.

Now be ready for a most important question. *Does your Sunday school provide these experiences?* If it does, your eights and nines are well on the way to a rich, full, Christian life.

If it does not, plan now to make changes necessary in establishing a teaching program that will provide for the needs of the children involved.

CHECK TASK—*Add to your "children's profile" notebook. Include materials which will help to illustrate the growth pattern of the eights and nines in the five areas which were discussed. Include descriptive phrases.*

CHAPTER THREE

5TH & 6TH GRADERS: PRETEEN PACESETTERS

OBJECTIVE—*to know and understand the physical, emotional, social, intellectual, and spiritual needs and characteristics of tens and elevens.*

Child or young adult? The ten and eleven year old child is struggling to balance himself somewhere between childhood and young adulthood. Does the teaching program in your church reflect this balance? Is there a change in the teaching plan as the child moves from the third and fourth grades to the fifth and sixth grades? As you read this chapter, list the changes that need to be made in your teaching plan to accommodate the needs of the growing ten and eleven year old.

PHYSICAL GROWTH

The ten year old child is usually very healthy. He has come through the age of communicable childhood diseases and is full of energy. Motor control is well developed, enabling him to participate in many "doing" activities with enthusiasm and success. He is willing to participate in activities involving both girls and boys. Girls have not yet reached the growth spurt which will put them temporarily ahead of the boys; therefore, they are both usually about the same height at this age.

The ten year old is at a point of rest or a plateau before the period of adolescence. It is an age of cooperation with adults.

Both ten and eleven year olds are active, curious, enthusiastic, honest and creative. They are interested in the world about them. They seek to experience a wide variety of things which are new and different.

Physical changes cause the eleven year old to tire easily. Many girls have started a physical growth spurt which will cause them to be taller than boys of the same age. Eleven year old boys are often restless and wiggly. They need to be able to explore and investigate to find answers to questions and problems. During this year, boys more often work and play with boys, while girls seek out other girls. Many times ten and eleven year olds would prefer to use the communication skills of talking, listening and reading rather than engaging in work activities. Consider how this fact will affect your plans for a class of tens and elevens on Sunday morning. How will it help you plan for during the week activities?

EMOTIONAL GROWTH

The ten year old has reached an emotional balance which causes him to be happy with himself. As a result, he is cooperative, easygoing, content, friendly and agreeable. Most adults enjoy working with this age group. The ten year old may evidence feelings of anger, but is quick to return to his happy self. Even though both girls and boys begin to think about their future as adults, their interests tend to differ at this point.

We also need to be aware of behavioral changes in the eleven year old. He is experiencing unsteady emotions and often shifts from one mood to another. He moves from sadness, dejection and anger, to happiness. We can frequently observe indications of jealousy or fear. He is easily drawn to tears. All of these emotions are a part of his journey from childhood to adulthood. His changes of feelings require patient understanding from the adults in his world. He needs to be able to make choices and decisions within the necessary limits that may be set by his peer group or adults.

The eleven year old will work for long periods of time and with concentration and enthusiasm on projects that are interesting and have meaning for him. He will often go far beyond the expectations set for him by adults. Have we provided for choices of activities which will be interesting and vital to our eleven year old?

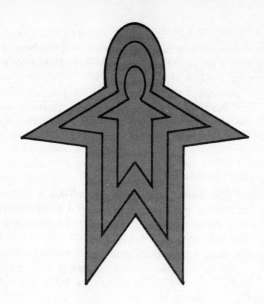

SOCIAL GROWTH

The ten year old has several centers for social activities. He is mainly concerned with family relationships, and values the judgments and feelings of his parents. He is anxious to be involved with his brothers or sisters in family excursions and projects. The ten year old also makes friends in his peer group quite easily. He likes to be a part of the group, but does not wish to be involved in competition. He does not want to stand apart for any reason. His ability to make valuable contributions to group activities is a beneficial experience for him. He can participate happily and with success in groups beyond the family cluster. Is your church providing many group activities for the ten year old? Are there both large and small group experiences? If not, what changes can you make that will bring about adequate group activities?

The eleven year old continues to value group activities. He is very likely to be an evaluator of the characteristics of the group members and is interested in maintaining the group code of behavior. Because of his desire to gain status for himself within his peer group, he will readily compete with others. Competition is even more intense when his group is involved in a contest, especially with a group of the opposite sex. This is all a part of finding a place in his world.

The eleven year old needs many group activities within his home, his school and his church. Let's not overlook these needs and fail to provide church-related group activities which will have meaning for the eleven year old.

INTELLECTUAL GROWTH

Consider the intellectual abilities and skills of the ten year old. He is very verbal. Talking, questioning and discussing need to be utilized in the teaching-learning plan. Ten year olds continue to be creative persons. They are able to express ideas and feelings through poetry, songs, drama, stories, drawing and painting. Stop and check the items which are included in your teaching plan for tens.

The ten year old is anxious to know the reasons for right and wrong. Making ethical decisions becomes a challenging task. He is eager to make right choices, but needs some help and guidance without too much direction.

The ten year old responds to visual stimuli. Consider carefully the number and kinds of visual aids used in your teaching plan for a pupil of this age. Abstract thinking and generalizations are still difficult for him to understand. He is still dealing with the concrete.

When he is eleven, he continues to internalize facts, specific information and concrete examples. He enjoys creating stories, poems, dramas, and working creatively with art materials. Roleplaying is a means of working out problems. The eleven year old is able to use this technique successfully and work through problem situations with resulting effective solutions.

The eleven year old begins to think of himself as an adult. He begins to read and question adult concepts. He is concerned about finding a place in the adult world. At this point, it seems to be an exciting change from the world of childhood. He sees himself as being able to determine things independently. Adult guidance must be available, but given in such a way that it will not destroy his efforts in becoming a thinking, self-directed person. The eleven year old is a reasonable person and will think through and accept logical conclusions.

As he becomes more keenly aware of his own feelings, desires and capabilities, he begins to develop definite ideas about his future. Boys may be considering the goals they have for jobs and professions, while girls may be concerned about marriage, a family or career possibilities. You can see that this is a very critical time in the growth pattern of a child. The roots of many important decisions are implanted at this age. God becomes a strong influence in choices that are being made for the thinking and planning of the future. The concern, understanding and guidance of Christian adults is extremely important, also. It is truly an awesome responsibility, as well as a great privilege, to be involved in the lives of these young people. Teachers can have a tremendous influence in the lives of tens and elevens, and their influence can be either positive or negative. Plan and prepare in such a way that your influence will be a positive one of lasting value.

Our tens and elevens continue to have many of the same needs and rights as the sixes, sevens, eights and nines. They still need to feel the love and understanding of concerned adults. It is important that they be encouraged to learn through involvement, action and discovery. The curriculum needs to be based upon the Bible for content, and upon opportunities for meaningful application to daily living. Tens and elevens are able to absorb Bible facts, and learning is not complete unless these facts can be translated into daily action. Caring teachers can bring about this necessary carry-over, through careful guidance of learning experiences.

SPIRITUAL GROWTH

Our understanding of tens and elevens can assist us in guiding meaningful experiences that will insure the greatest possible spiritual growth.

The ten year old is able to have deep feelings of love for God and an appreciation of God's love for him. He is aware of his need for a closeness with God through prayer and Bible reading, and often seeks to share his faith with his peer group. He is developing a sense of responsibility to his church. This may include the desire to be present for worship, to accept some responsibility for work within the church, or to be involved in service projects.

This is such an ideal time to encourage Bible reading. The ten year old can learn to use his Bible independently with success. He looks to God through the Bible for the guidance he needs in his daily life.

Tens are also able to bring increased skill, reasoning, and a widening background of experience to Bible learning activities. Since they are so concerned about family relationships, it is important to center our learning plan around the influence of the family. Bible learning and Christian worship need to be a part of the life of the family.

Our ten year old is eager to learn. He can assimilate factual material easily. We must use this time to deal with basic Bible facts to build a framework for understanding the Bible as it relates to daily life.

The learning plan for the Sunday school should include many opportunities for oral participation. Remember that the ten year old enjoys both oral activities and all kinds of creative activities. We must use these two areas continuously in our learning plan. The ten year old can be helped to become an integral part of the church program. He will become a participant in the activities which meet his needs and interests. He is able to understand the acceptance of responsibility to God through the church.

The eleven year old is able to grasp the relationship between God's love, His forgiveness, and our hope for eternal life more fully than the ten year old. He is aware of his need for God's forgiveness and his need for a personal Saviour. He seeks guidance from God when making important decisions in his life. He can understand God's plan for his life as revealed in the Bible. He begins to use Bible study tools, such as a concordance, a Bible dictionary, a commentary, and other related resource materials. Guidance in the selection and use of such study materials is important at this age.

He enjoys using the Bible to answer questions, to help with problems, and as a part of Bible learning activities.

Our eleven year old is an active participant in the group. Occasionally, activities need to be planned separately for boys and girls. At other times, both sexes will eagerly participate in the same activity. It is important that the church provide creative activities which involve physical action and which take the group out into the world. Opportunities should be given to satisfy the need of discovering answers and solutions.

Self-motivation becomes important. Demands from others do not provide adequate motivation for action. He needs help in dealing with feelings in a Christian way.

As we have considered the needs and characteristics of children from age six through eleven, we should remember that this composite picture will not describe any one given child. Herein lies the great challenge for the teacher. Think of Jesus and the examples of His teaching which are recorded in the New Testament. Jesus used the parable often as He taught in different places. He met the needs and differences of the people whom He taught. His examples were meaningful to the group with whom He was talking. An example used at one time was not appropriate at another time, in another place, or with a different group of people. We can learn from the Master Teacher the necessity of meeting the needs of our pupils.

CHECK TASK—*Add to your "children's profile" notebook. Include materials which will help to illustrate the growth pattern of tens and elevens in the five areas which were discussed. Include descriptive phrases.*

FOOTNOTES

PART I

CHAPTER 1

1 · Matthew 7:12, *The Living Bible,* Paraphrased. (Wheaton: Tyndale House, Publishers, 1971.) Used by permission.
2 · Ephesians 4:31,32, *TLB.*

PART II

SEE HOW THEY LEARN

CHAPTER FOUR

THE CHILD: A LEARNER

OBJECTIVE—*to begin to plan for meaningful learning experiences based upon information about the ways in which children learn.*

Learning is a continuous process that begins at birth and does not stop until death. A child learns as he lives. Every moment is filled with learning. Consider this concept in "Children Learn What They Live," by Dorothy Law Nolte.

CHILDREN LEARN WHAT THEY LIVE

If a child lives with criticism,
he learns to condemn . . .

If a child lives with hostility,
he learns to fight . . .

If a child lives with fear,
he learns to be apprehensive . . .

If a child lives with pity,
he learns to feel sorry for himself . . .

If a child lives with ridicule,
he learns to be shy . . .

If a child lives with jealousy,
he learns what envy is . . .

If a child lives with shame,
he learns to feel guilty . . .

If a child lives with encouragement,
he learns to be confident . . .

If a child lives with tolerance,
he learns to be patient . . .

If a child lives with praise,
he learns to be appreciative . . .

If a child lives with acceptance,
he learns love . . .

If a child lives with approval,
he learns to like himself . . .

If a child lives with recognition,
he learns that it is good to have a goal . . .

If a child lives with sharing,
he learns about generosity . . .

If a child lives with honesty and fairness,
he learns what truth and justice are . . .

If a child lives with security,
he learns to have faith in himself and in
those about him . . .

If a child lives with friendliness,
he learns that the world is a nice place
in which to live . . .

If you live with serenity,
your child will live with peace of mind. . . .[1]

Throughout the years of childhood, the learner is struggling to find his place in the world. He begins with the recognition of his own self-esteem, recognizes the worth of others, and then begins to accept the responsibility of working with others to function happily in his world. If the child is to grow happily and successfully, he must have the foundation that can be supplied only by effective Christian education based upon a love of and a faith in God.

How, then, can we pull together Bible facts, the needs of the child, and the environment for learning in which the child finds himself? We will first need to consider some of the goals of Christian education in relation to the growth of the learner.

GOALS FOR THE LEARNER

The learner is constantly in the process of change, brought about by his relationships with his fellow man and the world around him. Understandings, responses, and attitudes are always being developed. As new information and experiences come into the life of the learner, we can expect changes to take place which will lead to his fullest potential of growth.

However, meaningful growth and change in Christian education do not occur unless both long and short-range goals are set. These can be established by both learner and teacher. Pupils need to know the reasons for their study. They are interested in the "why" of their learning activities, as well as the "what." As the child grows in age and experience, his concern for learning objectives increases. The learner is usually eager to contribute some of his own objectives if he is given the opportunity.[2]

The highest general goals of Christian education are to help the student to believe in Jesus Christ through contact with the Word of God and meaningful learning experiences; to mature through the teachings of God's Word; and to live as an effective Christian in the world today, sharing Jesus Christ through word and deed. All learning experiences with children must lead to these general goals.

THE LEARNING PROCESS

How do these goals fit into the actual process of learning? In planning for activities appropriate to these aims, the teacher must have insight into some basic learning principles, as well as into the learning process itself. He must know how a child's background contributes to the learning situation and how to motivate his learners.

The learning process is a complex one. But it is essential for us to use what we know about learning if we are to guide boys and girls to a Christian life based upon their learning experiences with God's Word.

WHAT ARE SOME BASIC INSIGHTS INTO LEARNING?

Let's consider these factors which will be invaluable to us as church workers:

1   Learning goals that are meaningful to the learner will bring about effective learning.

2   Learning goals need to be realistic in their expectations. It should be possible to reach the goals with a reasonable amount of effort. The learner needs to be involved in the process of setting goals for himself.

3   Not all learning is planned learning. Children respond to the stimuli around them. Learning may occur at times and places quite unexpectedly.

4   Some learning is negative as well as positive. Not all change is desirable. Thinking processes, feelings, attitudes, and behavior may be changed in such a way as to bring about growth, or they may be changed in such a way as to hinder growth toward the Christian life.

5   Changes in observable behavior do not necessarily indicate a change in feelings and attitudes. The reverse is true. Not all inward changes in feelings, beliefs, and attitudes bring about an observable behavior change.

6   Not all learnings have the same significant value to the pupil. Values may change as the life situation of the learner changes from day to day.

7   Individual learning experiences are the most valuable when they are planned to meet the needs and interests of the learner. The readiness and capabilities of the learner must be considered.

8   Reinforcement is necessary if learning is to become an integral part of the life of the learner. Reinforcement may be brought about through practice, repetition, success, and appropriate reward. Failure and punishment for failure when honest effort is made may discourage and inhibit further effort. In some cases, failure may cause the learner to make a determined effort to bring about success. In general, learning experiences are positively reinforced with success.

We have been thinking about some basic concepts of learning that will help us make learning experiences more effective for our pupils. Let's concentrate now on actual steps in the learning process.

WHAT ARE THE STEPS IN THE LEARNING PROCESS?

How does a child actually learn? Learning involves much

more than the transmission of a collection of facts from the teacher to the learner. The learner must be at the center of the process. He must be the one who progresses from one step to another in the course of learning. No one can do it for him (#1).

Perception is the first step in the learning process. For a learner to receive and understand the information his teacher is presenting, there must be a common ground of communication (#2). The teacher must use a vocabulary and ideas familiar to the child so that he can perceive facts and insights on his level of understanding. Perception may also include the way a learner feels about the experience, or the way the learner places himself in relationship to the experience.

Problem solving involves the learner in the action response of making decisions and choices. The learner must consider several solutions to a problem (#3). Then, based upon his knowledge and experience, a decision is made and action taken. Following the action, evaluation is made of the outcome in terms of previously set goals.

Application comes about when concepts are translated into action in daily situations. If the pupil can apply what he has learned to his everyday relationships, the learning is meaningful and we can consider the process as being beneficial to the learner (#4). We should note, however, that even though the pupil has been able to make the application, learning does not stop there. New perceptions are formed and compared to old ones. New problems are solved on the basis of these fresh insights (#5). The true test of learning comes when a child uses what he has learned in new situations.

It is difficult to isolate these steps when teaching a class because each learner is progressing at his own rate. The pupil may be dealing with several concepts at once, each being on a different level of the learning process. Even though he may have applied the concept of honesty to his life, he may be at the problem solving stage in the concept of forgiveness. We as teachers need to be sensitive to a pupil's readiness to learn. Our prayerful attitude of encouragement can assist a pupil in accomplishing these steps.

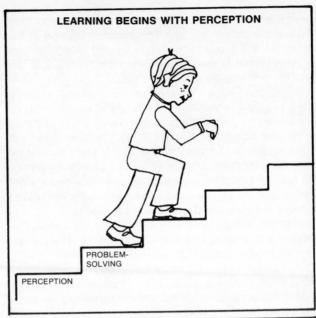

LEARNING BEGINS WITH PERCEPTION

PROBLEM-SOLVING

PERCEPTION

PERCEPTION

HONESTY

"Thou shalt not steal"

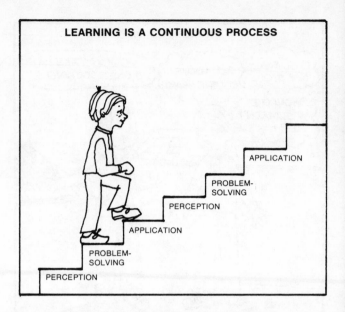

LEARNING IS A CONTINUOUS PROCESS

APPLICATION

PROBLEM-
SOLVING

PERCEPTION

APPLICATION

PROBLEM-
SOLVING

PERCEPTION

We can be thankful that God has given our pupils the capacity to learn. As God is a vital part of every phase of life, we can see Him as being an active part of the learning process. The goals which fit into the learning process need to be motivated so as to move the learner in the direction of God's will. God will be at work within the life of the learner through the Holy Spirit as He works through the church and the workers within the church program. The learner's faith, devotion, love, and forgiveness are strengthened as he moves through the learning process within the will of God.

WHAT DOES A CHILD'S BACKGROUND CONTRIBUTE TO LEARNING?

So far in this chapter, we have considered goals for learning, insights into learning, and the steps of the learning process itself. All these important factors can help contribute to our plans for effective learning experiences. But without knowledge of a child's background, our planning can be futile. What the child brings from his past and present environment can be of vital importance to the actual learning situation.

Let's consider these provoking questions. Has the child been a part of the church program all of his life? Is his family a part of the church? Will concepts from the church be strengthened with home teaching and activities? Will the child be encouraged throughout the week to apply to his daily life the teachings of the church? Is the Sunday school the only church contact the child has? What physical, mental, social, emotional, and spiritual needs has he brought to the learning situation? These questions point out the importance of the need to become thoroughly acquainted with each child.

Children of the same age or grade level come from a variety of environments and are vastly different from one another. No two children are alike or even very similar. You will need to determine how your time will be divided among your pupils so that you can glean information about them which will be of benefit to your planning. Our teaching program must also provide such a variety in methods and activities that the varying needs and differences of all the children within the class can be met.

Let's stop now to consider the information that you will want to have on hand about your learners. The sample worksheet might give you some ideas about the kinds of information you may wish to compile about each pupil. Complete an information sheet on each child. This can be accomplished in several ways. You may want to ask these questions in an informal gathering after church, or you might partially fill in the sheet after a home visit. Your pupils might enjoy writing their favorite Bible learning activities on 3 × 5 cards in the small group time after class. The data could then be transferred later to your information sheet.

Planning learning activities can be more effective if the information about each child is summarized on a Class Summary Sheet. A review of chapters 1-3 will assist you in becoming familiar with the characteristics and needs of your particular age group, and will enable you to fill in more accurately the areas concerning growth. When you have completed these charts, you will be able to plan a learning program that will help meet the needs of your specific group.

HOW CAN WE MOTIVATE LEARNING?

Motivation, or lack of it, has a direct relationship to the home environment of our learners, as well as to the learning situation itself. Knowledge of these factors can better equip us to provide effective motivation for our learners.

But just *how* do we motivate children to learn? What can we do to motivate a child from *within?* External motivation often does not lead to the most meaningful learning situations.

The most effective motivation comes when the learner feels that what he is learning can be related to immediate concerns in his daily life. He responds with eagerness and will work and struggle to acquire knowledge and/or skill. Teachers of children should take advantage of their natural curiosity and need for activity. Both are highly motivating forces which can be used positively.

Motivation devices that induce anxiety, fear, or pain, can be harmful to the learning process. Intense motivation may lead to emotionally distracting situations and cause learning to be less effective and meaningful.

Favorable learning occurs when it is accompanied by success rather than failure. Success will act as a strong reinforcement to learning and will provide a buffer for failure when it must occur.

A learning experience which will build up a child's self-esteem will lead to effective learning. Teachers need to know that children have the will to learn. They want to assimilate and use new information. They want to master new skills. They are curious and anxious to explore and discover the world around them. They are eager for opportunities to form many positive relationships with peer groups and adults. They are ready to become a part of a Christian education program which provides experiences and guidance through learning tasks that will bring a close relationship to God.

LET'S SUMMARIZE

We have thought through many important concepts about learning. To insure an effective learning process for children, let's condense into some brief guidelines what we know about it.

GOALS

1 Goals need to be set according to individual needs and capacities of children.

2 Goals should be established by both pupil and teacher.

3 Goals set should be within reach of the learner.

4 Children need to know what to look for when reading an assignment, viewing a film, or listening to recorded materials.

READINESS

1 Children learn when they are interested and ready. Capitalize on happenings, but also strive to create.

2 Acceptance by peer group and teacher causes a child to be more ready to learn.

3 Learners may need to be helped to interpret new materials, vocabulary, or concepts in relation to their own background or experience.

4 Children need to be allowed to learn at their own rate.

5 Encourage independence. Try not to do something for a child that he can do himself.

COMMUNICATION

1 The teacher does not need to talk in order for learning to take place. Learn to listen.

2 Children are very literal-minded. Words have only one meaning. Avoid the use of symbols.

3 Meaningful material is learned more quickly and is remembered longer.

4 Children are able to express ideas. They are receptive to the ideas of others.

5 Vocabulary used by the teacher should be on the child's level of understanding.

MOTIVATION

1 Take advantage of the child's drive for activity and his natural curiosity.

2 Be ready to shift activity and pace when the child's interest is waning.

3 Successful experiences bring about peak learning.

4 Using several senses in a learning situation will bring about more effective learning and action response.

5 Reinforced behaviors are likely to be repeated.

6 Learners avoid punishment and failure. They seek reward or success.

7 Allowing children to go on to other activities as they finish one assignment or learning experience will encourage them to complete a given task.

8 Children need to be encouraged to perform out of a desire to learn or a need to learn, rather than a desire for a symbol or mark of achievement.

9 Encourage creativity. Patterns or pictures to color have no educational value.

DISCIPLINE

1 Make suggestions rather than give commands. Use a positive approach to discipline.

2 Consistency is important to the learner.

3 Children can accept reasonable rules. They respond to simple organization.

ABILITIES

1 Children are capable of assuming roles of leadership or they may act as followers within the group. Opportunity should be provided for children to take on both roles.

2 Children are capable of participating in learning experiences that involve feelings, imagination, thinking, and decision making.

3 Children are able to participate in joint planning with other group members and the teacher.

MEETING NEEDS

1 Children need some freedom of choice and self-expression.

2 Children are full of energy. Continuous motion describes most children. They are developing physical skills. It is important to use this energy in learning activities.

3 Children like and need to help do things. They have a need to accept responsibility.

4 Children need opportunities to learn to think for themselves.

5 Children are curious. They question and reason. Their questions demand immediate answers.

6 The learner needs to feel the love of the teacher. A soft, clear voice is an indicator of love to the children.

7 It is not enough to determine a child's needs at one time and then consider that they will remain the same. Needs and interests change. We must be ever alert to these changes.

APPLICATION

1 Assist the learner in making a transfer of what he is learning to his daily living.

2 Relate new learnings to old.

Learning is so much more than the teacher imparting something of what he knows to the learner. The learner must be at the center of the learning process. Listening and responding to the Word of God brings about an awareness of God and His teachings. Awareness, then, is translated into action when the learner is involved with Bible learning activities. This will bring him in direct contact with the Christian faith and will require him to make decisions about the application of this faith to his life. This, after all, is the ultimate goal of Christian education.

CHECK TASK—*Establish an information sheet for each child in your Sunday school class. Begin to collect information about each child, record it, and consider it carefully during planning sessions. Select a child to observe. Watch the child you have chosen for about 15-20 minutes. List all of the different ways that your child used which brought about learning while you were a passive observer.*

CHAPTER FIVE

THE TEACHER: A LEARNING ENABLER

OBJECTIVE—*to discover the place of the teacher in God's plan; to try to add methods of home ministry.*

To be a teacher—what a choice responsibility in the family of God! What an important place God has given him in His plan! "Now ye are the body of Christ, and members in particular. And God hath set some in the church, first apostles, secondarily prophets, thirdly teachers. . . ."[1] "And he gave some, apostles; and some, prophets; and some, evangelists; and some, pastors and teachers; for the perfecting of the saints, for the work of the ministry, for the edifying of the body of Christ. . . ."[2]

What type of person must I be, to fill such a potential position? Let's look to Jesus, the Master Teacher. As He went from place to place, seeking teachers to work with Him, Jesus called a tax collector and fishermen. Paul, another biblical teacher, was a tentmaker. All can fit into God's plan for teaching.

WHAT CHARACTERISTICS SHOULD A TEACHER HAVE?

God expects us to develop some characteristics that will be of help to us as we encourage learners. Take some time now to consider these traits. Look to the Bible for guidance. Give prayerful consideration to each of these.

1 *Be enthusiastic*. A teacher with zeal, intensity and excitement, who does not let inhibitions rob him of the fullest expression of his real feelings and ideas, will

always have an audience. This does not mean being undignified, boisterous, or loud. Enthusiasm can be quiet, simple, controlled (Revelation 3:15,16; Romans 12:11).

2 *Have a sense of humor.* Playfulness is instinctive in the human being but is sometimes discouraged by the belief that it is sinful, or at best, childish. Certainly the Bible does not encourage frivolity, silliness, or lack of appropriate seriousness, but it points out that there is a place in the Christian life for laughter. It can be a healthy stabilizer and give balance to the serious aspects of the Christian life (Ecclesiastes 3:1,4; Psalm 126:2; Luke 6:21).

3 *Be careful of extremes.* It is true that sometimes life has "either/or" situations. For example, a man is a Christian or he is not. However, moderation is one of the key words in Christian living. Every good thing can have two undesirable extremes—too little of it and too much of it (Philippians 4:5, 1 Corinthians 9:25).

4 *Be a little ahead of the crowd.* One who does not stand out from the crowd in any way does not lead. A leader takes people from where they are to where he is. One must be willing to be a little different. However, if people feel that an individual is too different, too advanced or too radical, they do not follow him. Ezekiel stood ahead of the people of Israel and led them, yet he did not stand too far ahead. He "sat where they sat" [3] (see also Joseph in Genesis 37-50; Daniel; Nehemiah).

5 *Have variety in your personality.* A forceful and vigorous personality can be even more effective with an occasional "change of pace," such as a bit of restraint or outgoing thoughtfulness. An intense and serious personality can be more effective with an occasional bit of pleasant playfulness. A casual and calm personality can use a moment or two of special dignity. Variety is not only the spice of life, but it also gives color and effectiveness to personality (Ecclesiastes 3:1-8; Matthew 21:12,13 as compared with John 17; Acts 20:17-38).

6 *Appreciate beauty.* An appreciation of beauty can give richness, color and warmth to one's personality. A greater sensitivity to God who is the source of all

beauty can result in a greater joy in living. See the beauty not only of the big things, such as snowy mountains and rolling seas, but also of the little things in everyday life (Ecclesiastes 3:11; Psalm 27:4).

7 *Evaluate yourself honestly.* A Christian must guard against boastful pride, for everything we have is from God. Yet, on the other hand, we should not have an inferiority complex. We need to love others *as* ourselves. We should not belittle abilities, talents or accomplishments which God has given to us or to someone else. Nor should we overestimate talents and abilities (John 15:5; James 1:17; 1 Corinthians 1:30; Matthew 22:39).

8 *Train others to take responsibilities.* Consider Paul's ministry. He would stay in a town several years, if it took that long, to establish the work. When he was able to find people who could take over the leadership, he would put them in charge and go on. This principle is the key to successful, indigenous missions today. This principle applies to all Christian work, to secular business, to organizational activities and to many other phases of daily living. When an organization flourishes and goes on after a leader leaves, this shows that he has been a true leader. It is usually easier for one to do the job himself. But a real leader encourages, teaches and inspires others to take responsibilities (2 Timothy 2:2; 3:14,15).

9 *Use subtlety in relationships with others.* Some people "have their guard up," are skeptical, and hesitant to change from what they have always heard and practiced before. A straightforward, deductive personality, which tends to bring the issue to a head immediately and demands response, sometimes alienates others. Our personalities ought to be flexible enough to use a more subtle approach when the situation calls for it. Through the use of suggestion and gentle leading, we can often accomplish much more. Jesus, talking with the woman at the well, (John 4:3-26), illustrates this point. Other parables demonstrate this. Some of Paul's sermons also use this method (Acts 13:14-44; Acts 17:15-34).

10 *Strive for mental directness in relationships with others.* Each person must feel that you are dealing personally with him. Consider the ministry of Jesus. Think

about the highly individualized responses of the apostles at the Last Supper. When someone is talking to you, look him in the eye and really listen! When you are talking to individuals or to an audience, establish direct eye contact. Think about the individual and how the meaning of your words is influencing his mind and heart and life (John 13:4-26).

WHAT ARE THE TEACHER'S RESPONSIBILITIES?

Let's reflect a few moments on the awesome responsibility of a teacher. What do you think he should be—a communicator of facts and knowledge? The planner and provider of learning activities? Or, the organizer of time and space?

HELP YOUR PUPILS LEARN

The basic responsibility of the teacher is to enable the pupil to learn; thus, the teacher—a learning enabler! In order to be an effective learning enabler in the education program of the church, we must be so filled with the love of God that our pupils can feel His great love through us.

Think back to your years of association with learning enablers. Remember the teacher that meant the most in your life. The one you remember most clearly probably really loved you and cared for you. You were recognized as a valuable individual. Your needs were met. Self-esteem developed as you felt secure in the love and concern of this effective teacher.

Creating such a healthy climate for learning is most important in the life of a child whose only contact with the church is through his teacher. He, along with the child who has many church contacts, needs security. The example and actions of the Sunday school worker have far more impact on the child than the words that are said through the teaching program. The teacher is influencing his pupils both consciously and unconsciously. Children perceive much through feeling and observation. Fortunate is the child whose teacher can say, "Be ye followers of me, even as I also am of Christ."[1]

The teacher will also need to help his pupils learn by providing opportunities for involvement, planning, doing, and evaluating. These opportunities should allow for discovery and exploration of real situations. A variety of learning experiences needs to be planned. Children are able to participate in the planning. The learning enabler will stimulate the child to think and reason for himself. He may act as an interpreter of shared experiences. He will help to lift out and clarify pupils' thoughts.

The learning enabler will follow the child's lead, taking him from where he is to new areas of understanding. He will need to guide learning experiences, not just speak facts and concepts. The child's total life will need to be considered when planning for him. We cannot isolate the child from the world about him. Everything that we know about the way children learn, should encourage us to involve the child in a variety of experiences. Just sitting in rows, and listening to the teacher does not bring about meaningful learning.

KNOW YOUR PUPILS IN THE GROUP

The learning enabler needs to learn as much about the pupils as possible. This responsibility includes learning about them as a group and about each individually. Consider ways to accomplish this.

Learning about pupils as a group can be brought about through reading available materials about needs, characteristics and learning patterns of the age group with which we work. Eager participation in training opportunities can bring about a helpful understanding of our pupils. Perhaps the most direct way to learn about children is to become involved with them in their activities.

KNOW YOUR PUPILS INDIVIDUALLY

Of equal importance to age group understanding is knowing as much as possible about each pupil specifically. It is important for the Sunday school worker to plan carefully for additional contact with each pupil, over and above that which occurs at church on Sunday morning. Visiting in the child's home and neighborhood are obvious places to gain needed information and understanding. Find out about the child's place in his family. Discover the kinds of school experiences that are a part of the child's life. Learn to know the strengths and weaknesses of each child. Find out about special needs that may be related to spiritual, emotional, social, intellectual, and physical growth. Plan for outings with a small group of children so that each may have a good share of your love and interest. A visit to your home by a few pupils at a time brings about a closer relationship between teacher and pupil.

MINISTER TO YOUR PUPILS

Consider your ministry to the children within your class. As you become better acquainted with your pupils, you will discover many special ways to minister to their needs. Think about including some of these in your schedule this week.

Ministry is . . .

Taking a child for a doctor's appointment for a working mother.

Child-sitting while parents house hunt.

Setting a little girl's hair so she will feel pretty.

Sitting with a sick baby while Mother takes a breather or goes grocery shopping.

Praising a child for the way he handles his crutches.

Giving a birthday party for a child of migrant workers and keeping in touch by letters when the family has moved on.

Teaching a motherless child to sew on buttons.

Making special efforts to attend the music recitals and school plays of the children in your class.

Cultivating friendships with children who seem to have no present needs, for someday they may need you.

Helping a child live through the time of a broken dream.

Helping a child face the death of a loved one by allowing moments of tender sadness and by using conversation to prevent the development of misconceptions because adults in his family are caught in periods of depression.

Allowing children to talk and talk and talk.

Helping children and parents feel that there are persons who believe in them and will help them to find the strength and support that Christian friends can give.[5]

The responsibility of ministry should not be that of the learning enabler alone. Children must also minister to others according to their age level, capabilities, and spiritual development. Here is where the teacher can assist children in such learning experiences. She might first want to share Matthew 25:40 where Jesus said, "Verily I say unto you, Inasmuch as ye have done it unto one of the least of these my brethren, ye have done it unto me."[6] Then she might assist her pupils in thinking of ways to help other people. She can encourage a four or five year old to think of a number of things that he can do to help a sad friend or a person who is ill. Children will enjoy the opportunity of going with their teacher to visit another child. They are eager to be of help to those about them. They will respond eagerly to the friendly guidance of their teacher and can be reminded of the verse in Hebrews, "Don't forget to do good and to share what you have with those in need, for such sacrifices are very pleasing to Him."[7]

The responsibility of the teacher is indeed a great one. Know that you are not alone in the acceptance of this responsibility. Other workers in the department, the learning enabler, the child's home, and most important, the learner himself, are all a part of the learning team.

Be grateful for the opportunity that God has given through the blessed privilege of guiding the learning of children in the education program of the church. "I thank him who has given me strength for this, Christ Jesus our Lord, because he judged me faithful by appointing me to his service."[8]

CHECK TASK—*Choose the teacher characteristics which you would like to work on during the next few months. Post a list in a prominent place, study the Scripture references, then begin to work consistently on improvement of that characteristic.*

Contact at least one of the pupils who was not present. Following one of the suggestions given, or another that you feel would meet the needs of a child, use at least one new method and evaluate the effectiveness of the contact.

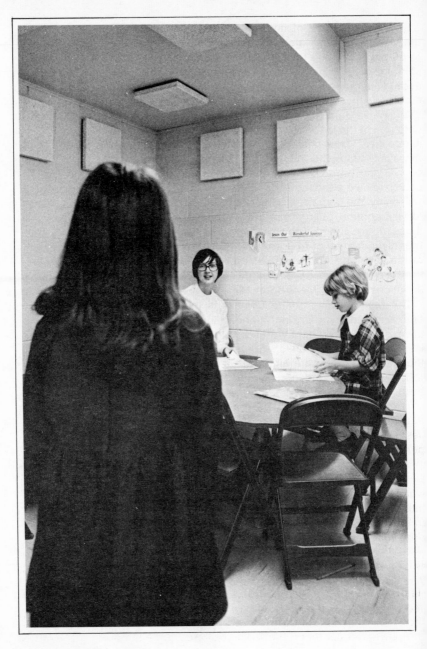

CHAPTER SIX

SET THE STAGE FOR LEARNING

OBJECTIVE—*to put together the elements of space and equipment in such a way as to provide a suitable environment for rich and meaningful learning experiences.*

When the learner and learning enabler are brought together in a healthy learning climate, the stage is ready for dynamic learning experiences. But what contributes to a healthy environment such as this? How can we use our surroundings to the best advantage for effective learning?

Jesus found it possible to teach effectively in whatever place He found Himself. He used the natural surroundings to stimulate learning. As we think of Jesus' use of a wide variety of experiences, can we find a way to use this concept within the confines of the walls of our classrooms? The answer is obvious. We need to bring into our classrooms informality, some of the spaciousness of the outdoors, and the flexibility necessary to meet the moment-by-moment needs of the learners. As the learner interacts with his environment, other learners, and teachers, he is able to discover and bring together those experiences which have meaning for him at a particular moment.

The learner needs to be an active participant in the learning experiences. Learning is not passive. It does not magically occur when there is quiet and apparent concentration on the part of the pupil. Learning does not always occur when the teacher shares some informatior with the learner. Children need to feel a freedom of movement, expression and exploration, if real and meaningful learning is to take place.

ARRANGING THE BACKDROPS

When a child walks into a room, it says something to him. It may be positive or negative. Look at the room in which you teach. If you teach a first or second grade class, you may wish to go into the room on your knees. Check the room from the eye level of the child. As you look around the room in an objective manner, answer some evaluative questions.

1   How do you feel about entering the room?

2   Is the room neat and clean?

3   Is the room colorful, light and warm?

4   Is there something that is attractive to you?

5   Is there a spot of beauty?

6   Do you feel encouraged to become involved in some activity?

7   Do you feel free to talk with others who may be in the room?

8   Is there an activity you can do alone if you do not want to work with another person?

9   Can you choose a quiet activity or one that will involve more physical involvement?

10   Can you find the materials that you need?

11   Is there space enough to move around?

12   Is the furniture and equipment useful, flexible and comfortable for the age group that will be using it?

13   If you do not have enough room, what can be removed to give more space?

14   Is there another way that the furniture and equipment might be placed to allow more room and flexibility in the program?

As you answer these questions, there may be some things that you wish to do in your room that will cause it to become a more suitable environment for learning. It will probably not be possible to accomplish all of your goals at once. Make a priority list and move through it as you are able. Perhaps there will be little or no funds available to purchase needed supplies, equipment or repairs. Once again, do those things which are possible for you to do and work around those things which you cannot change.

As you plan for the kinds of learning experiences that you feel are most appropriate for your pupils, you may find that the room is not as flexible as you would like it to be. You may prefer to use open rooms with several learning centers. If your building provides only a large assembly room with small classrooms adjoining it, consider removing some nonessential walls, or using the smaller classrooms with doors open as work spaces for a variety of learning activities. If your church is in the process of building or remodeling an educational unit, be sure that the building committee is well aware of the teaching philosophy which is the basis of your education program. If it is necessary for you to use existing buildings, you will find that there are many ways to adapt the existing construction to the teaching program that best suits your church.

Diagram 1

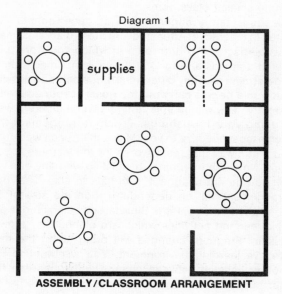

ASSEMBLY/CLASSROOM ARRANGEMENT

Diagram 2

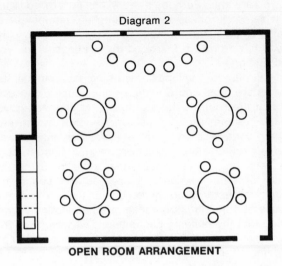

OPEN ROOM ARRANGEMENT

Look at diagrams 1 and 2. In diagram 1, you will see an arrangement of an assembly room with several adjoining smaller classrooms.

A suggested arrangement for an open room is illustrated in diagram 2. After studying these diagrams, make several diagrams of the room in which you work. First sketch it as it is arranged at the present time. Then try to determine as many different arrangements as possible that would help to carry out the goals of your education program. You will be able to find several different ways of using your furnishings. Try the arrangement that seems most effective to you. Make shifts each week until you find a way that really works for the learners in your class. Now don't become so satisfied with any one way that you do not change it from time to time. The room arrangement will be dependent upon the size of the room, attendance pattern, Bible lesson being taught, and Bible learning activities which are planned for a given session. Frequent changes will bring about the most effective learning environment. You will want to find enough balance between change and routine so that your pupils can be flexible and still feel secure.

The amount of space provided for a classroom is a very important consideration. Many churches have an educational unit with many small rooms. As a result, pupils are crammed into limited space. However, the rationale behind this situation is usually for the learners to have a close relationship with peer groups and with the learning enabler.

The opposite extreme is a church which provides very large rooms. Larger groups of pupils are assigned to each room. Sometimes the class size is from 50 to 100 pupils. In both cases, learning is usually not at peak level and teachers and pupils may become tired and frustrated with the situation. Therefore, the effectiveness of the total program is limited.

Chamberlain and Fulbright, in their book *Children's Sunday School Work,* suggest several questions that you may wish to ask yourself. The answers will help to determine the space needs for your department.

Answer the questions *Yes* or *No*.

1 Is the room at least 20 by 30 feet?_____

2 Is the room no larger than 25 by 30 feet?_____

3 Does the room provide 25 square feet of floor space for each person (workers and pupils) enrolled?_____

4 Does the room open into a main corridor?_____

5 If there are other children's departments, is your room located near them?_____

6 Are toilet facilities accessible?_____

7 Is there a drinking fountain nearby?_____

8 Are windows of clear glass low enough for the children to see through easily?_____

9 Is there sufficient wall space for such items as large pieces of equipment, a picture rail and a tackboard and a chalkboard?_____[1]

As you evaluate, determine which items of need you can change at this time. Then set about to make the desirable changes. If there are items that you cannot change but need attention, share your evaluation with others who may be able to assist in bringing about a more effective learning environment.

There are some adjustments that you can make yourself. Take a good look at the bulletin board and chalkboard in your room. Are these areas at the eye level of the learners? Is the material placed on them conducive to learning? If the answer to these questions is no, you can make the desirable changes.

Is your room dark and dingy? You, together with interested parents, can paint the walls and ceiling. Furnishings in need of paint or repair can be made more usable with the combined efforts of parents and teachers. If the furnishings in your class are too large or too small, survey the equipment in all of the departments. You may be able to exchange furniture so that more than one group will benefit and receive furniture of the correct size. If this is not possible, find a carpenter in the church. Adjustment of chairs and tables to correct heights will not be a difficult task for someone with carpenter's skill.

The most important concept when thinking about space for learning is that the room itself teaches. Feelings and concepts taught can have more lasting value if they are enhanced with appropriate surroundings.

EQUIPPING THE STAGE

If your stage for learning is to be effective, it will be necessary to select materials and equipment with care. If space is at a premium, consider which items of furniture can be removed. If you have a piano, can it be taken out and an Autoharp, guitar, zither or melody bells used in its place? Can some of the tables be removed? Most of the activities which usually take place on tables can be done on the walls or on the floor. Many times younger children are content to sit on a rug or carpeted floor area. This will allow the removal of some of the chairs. Stop and think! Is it really necessary for all of the class members to sit on chairs at any one given time? If not, perhaps it will be possible to remove additional chairs.

If the space available to you is adequate, think about the arrangement of the furnishings and equipment in such a way as to use the space to the greatest advantage. You may wish to work with the flexibility that square and trapezoidal tables permit. Round tables offer opportunities for creative use of space. Such items as book rack, coat rack, shelves (both closed and open), storage cabinets, paint racks, easels, chalkboards, and bulletin boards all need to be considered as valuable aids to learning. It is possible to improvise with much of this equipment when funds are not readily available for purchase.

A piece of fiberboard, leaning against or hanging from the wall, will serve as a satisfactory substitute for the commercially purchased and installed bulletin board area. Paint easels may be easily and inexpensively made by tying together two pieces of 30" × 30" pegboard at the top with sturdy cord. Tie them together at the bottom, also, leaving about six inches of cord between the boards. This will produce a tentlike easel which will stand on a table or on the floor. One child can work on each side at the same time. A shoe box will serve as a satisfactory paint rack. Some teachers have successfully used mug racks to hang wraps. Use some time, some ingenuity, and a group of project-minded parents and/or some church members to complete many of the items that will be needed for an enriching learning environment.

We have combined the learners, the learning enabler, the space, the equipment and materials. Now we are ready to lift the curtain on the stage of learning, which, if properly prepared, should result in meaningful learning experiences.

CHECK TASK—*Diagram your classroom as it is now. Make a new diagram. Indicate changes which you can make that will increase the effectiveness of the learning. Establish a priority list of needed equipment. Be sure to recognize those items that cannot be changed, and begin to work with those that may be changed.*

CHAPTER SEVEN

READY, GO!

OBJECTIVE—to understand the steps necessary in initiating an effective plan for successful learning experience.

The learner, the teacher, the space, and the equipment are all ready! There must be a plan of organization in order for them to fit together like the pieces of a puzzle. We cannot leave it to chance. A careful plan must go into effect if the desired outcomes are to be achieved.

How can we plan in such a way that the situations of many different churches in many different areas will be met? We will attempt to offer alternate plans which will meet a variety of needs. Select the one that most nearly fits into the situation in which you find yourself. The plans are flexible so that you may bring about the necessary changes to insure success for your children.

The task of planning to guide and encourage the learning experiences of children brings with it a privilege and a great responsibility. We must enter into planning and preparation with prayer. Read Ephesians 6:18, "With all prayer and petition pray at all times in the Spirit. . . ."[1]

Think about your teaching situation. Then examine the two suggested plans on pages 60 and 61. Both plans incorporate Bible study and Bible learning activities and allow some time for the large group as well as time for small groups. After carefully examining Plan A and its three blocks of time and Plan B with two blocks of time, have your staff select the plan most suitagle to your situation.

PLAN A

HOW TO USE YOUR TOTAL SESSION TEACHING TIME

BIBLE STUDY	BIBLE SHARING/ PLANNING	BIBLE LEARNING ACTIVITIES
This diagram represents the first block of time for the Sunday school period. It includes all the material to be used in the permanent class grouping. When the child arrives, he begins working on an activity that builds readiness for Bible learning. He then listens to the Bible story and thinks through ways of applying to his own life the truths he learned from God's Word.	This diagram represents the time when all the children in the department are together in a large group. Normally it will be the second time block in the Sunday school hour. All the children share together in worship and other large group activities. Then each child selects the Bible learning activity he wants to work on during the third block of time.	This diagram represents the block of time which normally is the last portion of the Sunday school period. Children are divided into small nonpermanent groups, according to the activities they choose to work on. A teacher leads each activity. Note that at this time the teacher does not work with his own class group, but rather with the children who choose the activity he is leading.

If you have 75 minutes

25-35 minutes	up to 15 minutes	20-25 minutes

If you have 60 minutes

25-30 minutes	up to 10 minutes	20 minutes

Note: *For review purposes of each unit, the last two blocks of time can be reversed —children go directly from class time to their Bible learning activities; then all could meet together for large group time. This would allow children to complete their Bible learning activities (small groups) and then to share what they learned during the unit (large group).*

PLAN B

ANOTHER WAY OF USING THE LESSON MATERIAL

BIBLE STUDY/BIBLE LEARNING ACTIVITIES 40 minutes (permanent class group)	BIBLE SHARING 15-20 minutes (department group)
Teacher uses suggestions in Bible Study time and chooses one Bible learning activity for his entire class to take part in.	Department Superintendent adapts material from Bible Sharing/Planning section. Music and conversation are thus an outgrowth and/or expression of what was learned in class time. Note that it will not be necessary to allow for planning and choosing Bible learning activities when material is arranged in this way.

After your staff has selected the most suitable plan (either Plan A, B, or an adaptation of the two plans) it will be necessary to take the next step in planning. In order to have effective learning on Sunday morning the department staff must pull together the many details involved in the Sunday morning hour.

Before the beginning of each unit it will be important to have a staff meeting for planning purposes. Make specific plans for each block of time you plan to use on Sunday morning. Review the charts on these pages with your staff and make sure that each staff member understands the purpose and goals of each block of time.

Three Worksheets are available to help you make plans at your staff meeting. Worksheet #1 should be used by the department superintendent to plan the total program of the unit. By completing the first sheet at the staff meeting you will make sure that you are covering every detail that needs to be covered at that time. Worksheet #2 and #3 will be used by the individual teacher to plan for the total program for which he is responsible each week.

AT THE STAFF MEETING

1 Have each staff member become familiar with the unit in your Sunday school curriculum. Become familiar with the unit aim as well as the lesson aims.

2 Examine the suggestions in the teacher's manual for the activities suggested for building readiness in Bible learning.

3 Discuss the role of the teachers and the department superintendent so that each will be clear concerning their respective duties.

4 Carefully discuss how you will use the hour.

5 Discuss the Bible learning activities which will be used.

6 Make tentative plans for how the unit will be completed and what type of evaluation you plan to have.

Now that your staff meeting is completed you are ready for Sunday morning.

ON SUNDAY MORNING

The description below is based on Plan A (three blocks of time). If you choose to use Plan B (two blocks of time) adapt the material below to fit that schedule.

Bible Study — During this time the children are in a small permanent class group. When the child arrives he begins working on an activity that builds readiness for Bible learning. Then the student listens to the Bible story and thinks through ways of applying the truths he has learned from God's Word to his own life.

The small permanent class group (the first block of time) should be made up of approximately six learners and one teacher. The opportunity for the learners to closely identify with one adult will be brought about through this permanent class group.

In preparation for the small group time, the teacher will need to think through the purposes for the unit as provided in the curriculum materials. In addition to those stated, he may wish to add others which will help to meet specific needs of the children in this group.

Bible Sharing/Planning — The large group time (the second block of time) should involve the total department. Attendance should not exceed 25-30. The purpose of the large group time will be to share and plan for Bible learning activities. Some worship experience will be planned for this time.

During this group planning session it is necessary to recall the Bible material related to the activity. The meaning that the learner will take to the activity is dependent upon the Bible material and upon its application to his life. The learner will choose an activity he will work on in the Bible Learning Activity period. Some activities will extend throughout the unit, others will be completed in one session. The curriculum materials provide suggestions for both continuous unit activities and weekly activities.

When selecting the activities suggested in the curriculum for your group consider the sophistication of the group of children with whom you are working. Many first and second grade children have difficulty in remembering and making a carry-over from Sunday to Sunday. If this is true of your group you will want to plan for weekly activities. Third, fourth, fifth, and sixth grade children are more able to work through a continuous activity which lasts for the length of the unit. With many groups.

Bible Learning Activities — The nonpermanent groups (the third block of time) will permit the learner to work with a peer group of his choice. He will make this selection on the basis of interest in the activity for that group.

The prime responsibility of each activity leader is to guide the children in planning and carrying out their selected Bible activity. The learners who have chosen to work on a weekly activity may immediately begin work on that activity.

The learners who have chosen a continuing unit activity will have opportunity for additional decision making. They will first of all decide how best to launch their project, what they want to accomplish, and then *who will do what part.* Abilities and talents of the learners will complement one another . . . some students will do the art work, for example, while others do the research.

CHECK TASK—Select one of the plans in this chapter and adapt it to your church needs.

TOTAL SESSION UNIT PLAN SHEET

(Bible Study, Bible Sharing/Planning, Bible Learning Activities*)

Title of Unit: _____ Dates:_____

Bible passages: _____

Persons and/or events in Bible passage: _____

Unit aim: That the students may (know, feel):

That the students may respond by:

Bible verses to know: _____

Songs to teach: _____

BIBLE STUDY* (Each teacher fills out worksheet #2 after department staff meeting)

BIBLE SHARING/PLANNING*

Date	Program for the day	Materials for superintendent

BIBLE LEARNING ACTIVITIES*

Activity	Teacher
1. _____	_____
2. _____	_____
3. _____	_____
4. _____	_____
5. _____	_____

*Based on the three blocks of time in teacher's/leader's manual.

Worksheet #2 (Each teacher uses this sheet to plan his specific responsibilities *after department staff meeting.*)

TEACHER UNIT WORKSHEET FOR *BIBLE STUDY*

Specific prayer requests/student needs to be met:

BUILDING READINESS ACTIVITIES			BIBLE STUDY		
Date Lesson	Activity	Materials	Scripture	Lesson Aims	Questions to relate Bible lesson to life
			Bible passage Bible characters and/or events Bible verse to know		
			Bible passage Bible characters and/or events Bible verse to know		
			Bible passage Bible characters and/or events Bible verse to know		
			Bible passage Bible characters and/or events Bible verse to know		
			Bible passage Bible characters and/or events Bible verse to know		

Worksheet #3   (Each teacher uses *one sheet per Bible Learning Activity* for which he will be responsible. Fill this sheet out *after* department staff meeting.)

TEACHER WORKSHEET FOR
BIBLE LEARNING ACTIVITIES

Bible Learning Activity: _____

Date(s): _____   For unit sharing? _____

Purpose: _____

_____

Materials: _____

_____

Procedures: _____

_____

Children who choose this activity: Responsibility:

1. _____   _____

2. _____   _____

3. _____   _____

4. _____   _____

5. _____   _____

6. _____   _____

7. _____   _____

8. _____   _____

FOOTNOTES

PART II

CHAPTER 4

1 · Dorothy Law Nolte. "Children Learn What They Live." (Los Angeles: The American Institute of Family Relations, n.d.)
2 · Lois Curley. "Where Am I Going? And How Will I Know if I'm on the Way?" *Teach Magazine.* (Glendale: G/L Publications, Winter, 1970), p. 39.

CHAPTER 5

1 · I Corinthians 12:27,28, King James Version.
2 · Ephesians 4:11,12, *KJV.*
3 · Ezekiel 3:15, *KJV.*
4 · I Corinthians 11:1, *KJV.*
5 · "Ministry Is for Children's Workers Too." Prepared by Mrs. A. A. Westbrook. (Nashville: Sunday School Board, Southern Baptist Convention, n.d.)
6 · Matthew 25:40, *KJV.*
7 · Hebrews 13:16, *The Living Bible,* Paraphrased. (Wheaton: Tyndale House, Publishers, 1971). Used by permission.
8 · I Timothy 1:12, *Revised Standard Version.* From RSV of the Bible, copyrighted 1946 and 1952 by the Division of Christian Education of the NCCC, U.S.A., and used by permission.

CHAPTER 6

1 · Eugene Chamberlain and Robert G. Fulbright. *Children's Sunday School Work.* (Nashville: Convention Press, 1969), p. 146.

CHAPTER 7

1 · Ephesians 6:18, *American Standard Bible.* (La Habra, Calif.: The Foundation Press Publications, 1971.)

PART III

SEE THEM IN ACTION

CHAPTER EIGHT

WORKERS TOGETHER WITH GOD

OBJECTIVE—*to understand the importance of Bible learning activities in the Sunday school program.*

PLAN ACTION FOR GOD'S ACTIVE CHILDREN

Cooperating with God in an effort to implement His ideas into our learning situation can be exhilarating! We are His instruments as we put our insights to work—insights we have gleaned from our study of children, of the learning enabler, and of the learning process itself.

In our total learning program, we can use God's example of creativity and variety for effective teaching methods. We can use His gift of the five senses so that children will better know Him. We can use the distinct feature of activity which God has bestowed on children for more effective learning. We are "God's fellow-workers"[1] in the building of His Church.

It doesn't take a learning enabler long to discover that children are always on the move. Young children especially cannot be still for extended periods of time. We must not only allow activity, but we must plan carefully so that the activity which occurs will be related to meaningful learning. Listen to the conversation of children. What do these comments tell you about the success and happiness of children in church?

"Do I have to do it now?"

"Is it time to go already?"

"I like this class. You get to *do* things."

"Nothing is any good to do, unless you can be messy!"

"You don't have to color, you can do anything you want!"

"I wish we could come again tomorrow."

"Can I really make it look any way I want to?"

These are comments of children working together in a classroom which provides Bible learning activities. Some of them are surprised that they really can make some choices. This is a new church experience for many children. Some are unaware of how quickly time passes when they are happily engaged in pursuits of their choice which meet their needs and interests. Some are pleased because they can really "do things." The looks of joy, happiness, concentration and learning are difficult to describe. We have established that learning takes place when there is accompanying activity. What better way is there for a child to experience the teachings of Jesus about loving others than to become involved in a project that helps them to share with others. We learn to love and to share by experiencing loving and sharing.

USE THE METHODS OF JESUS

Our activities can be more meaningful if we follow Jesus' example in meeting the needs of the learners. Jesus often used objects to help teach a lesson so that it would have meaning for His hearers. Jesus knew that looking at an object during a lesson would help to impress it upon the minds of the learners. When the disciples needed a lesson about the idea of faith, Jesus used a ready example—the fig tree (Matthew 21:18-22). At another time, when Jesus was questioned about paying taxes, He took a coin with the image of Caesar and said, "Render therefore unto Caesar the things which are Caesar's; and unto God the things that are God's."

Jesus used parables as well as objects. In Mark 4:3-8, we read of the sower who went forth. The seed is likened to the Word of God. The crowd by the sea that day was familiar with the properties of seeds and their needs for growing. They could easily make the transfer to the growing of God's Word within the heart of man.

Think of the symbolism of the Last Supper and the drama that it portrayed. Jesus was aware of the impact that this dramatic event would have in the lives of those about Him. Read Matthew 26:17-29.

Jesus met each learner at his own particular point

of need. The learning/teaching method used was the most appropriate for that person at that moment. Remember several instances when He used a discussion or question and answer method. One instance that comes quickly to mind is His discussion with the Samaritan woman at the well. She was guided to discover who Jesus was through careful discussion. Read John 4:7-26.

We can read of occasions when Jesus found the lecture method to be effective. Perhaps the one which comes most quickly to mind is the Sermon on the Mount. Jesus often spoke to large crowds of people in many different settings. Each time, the learners were blessed by their contact with the Master Teacher. Read the Sermon on the Mount as it is recorded in Matthew 5, 6 and 7. Even though it is a continuous sermon or lecture, notice the many ways in which Jesus presented the truth during that one lesson.

Plan to follow the example of Jesus and involve learners in as many different learning experiences as possible. Plan to meet the needs of the children. The methods you choose will depend upon the learner, the subject, the time and the place. Make the most of every opportunity to guide the learning of a child.

UTILIZE A CHILD'S FIVE SENSES

Use the five senses God created in your pupils. Plan activities which will help your learners utilize these senses in his exploration of the world. This can best be accomplished if your lessons are not all confined to the classroom. A child can better understand God as Creator of the universe if he spends time in the out-of-doors. As he looks about himself in wonder, will he not be able to see the greatness of God? As he listens to the sweet singing of the birds and the gentle rustle of the wind through the trees, will he not feel the presence of the God who loves him and created a world to be his home?

Looking and listening will not be adequate if we wish to be certain that the child truly appreciates God's creation. Think of knowing God through the touch of a kitten's soft fur, the feel of sand and mud between wriggling toes, the sensation of the sea anemone gently closing around a fingertip.

The fragrance of the rosebud, the smell of new-fallen leaves, the salty sea air, and freshly cut grass all communicate to the child the grandness of God's creation.

Very often, the child's sense of taste is overlooked when we plan for the teaching of God's Word. Stop now and make a list of opportunities you can see for using the sense of taste. Imagine the learner beginning to feel as if he were with Jesus as a boy. He might begin to understand something of Jesus' life as he tastes the fig, almond, cheese, olive, or bread dipped in honey. The child will feel with the multitude as he has a taste of fish and loaves. The wonder of the miracle of Jesus will become a very real part of his life. The feelings of the widow and Elijah will be shared as children participate in the baking and eating of simple cakes.

As learning enablers, we are working with the total child—one who has five senses and an almost endless amount of energy to explore the world about him. If we are to work with the total child, our planning must include opportunities for each part of the child's learning system to function. Put the child together. We cannot work effectively with only a portion of this living being.

BE CREATIVE IN PLANNING

If our goals for learning are to be met, the activities we plan must be creative. Elizabeth Allstrom, in her book *You Can Teach Creatively,* describes the creative teacher. The creative learning enabler

—captures and holds the pupils' interest with materials gleaned from many sources—all relating to their daily living.

—is relaxed. He has time for laughter, for conversation, for getting to know them, for finding ways to share himself with them. His eyes and interests are ever on the children.

—has confidence that the wisdom within each child will enable him to handle his own behavior.

—encourages original work, both from their minds and from their hands and lets them feel his confidence in their ability to do it.[3]

PUT THE CHILD TOGETHER!

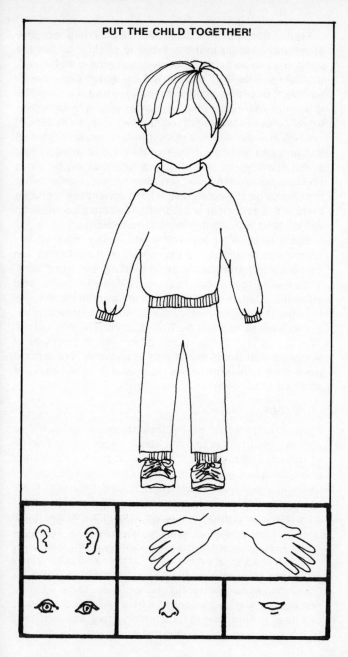

For purposes of this discussion, let us think of "creative" as meaning that the learning enabler allows the child to do some of the thinking and planning for himself. In other words, the activity will be accompanied with sufficient direction and guidance to insure a successful learning experience, but the learner will have an opportunity to produce something that is uniquely a part of himself. He will have the opportunity to express his own thinking and feelings. This expression is an integral part of the learning process. Creative activities will help our children become thinking, creative people, instilled with the teachings of God's Word. These concepts will enable them to live as concerned Christians within a fast-moving world, filled with confusion and contradiction.

Begin to think of yourself as a creative learning enabler. With assurance of God's help and guidance, you can enter into the adventure of guiding learning experiences among children. Look to God for help and strength. "Call unto me, and I will answer thee, and show thee great and mighty things, which thou knowest not."[4]

Be ready to share a part of yourself with each child. "So, being thus tenderly and affectionately desirous of you, we continued to share with you not only God's good news (the Gospel) but also our own lives as well, for you had become so very dear to us."[5]

BE SELECTIVE IN CHOICE

If we can agree that we need to provide creative activities, our next task is to think about the variety or choice of activities that will be needed in a classroom at any given time. Is it enough to provide one creative activity? Let's answer that question with another. Will it be enough to interest only some of the children? No matter how interesting and inviting an activity might be, it will not meet the needs of every child within the class. All children will not learn from the same experience.

Not all children are developing at the same rate. Within one class of children we will find variations in muscular development, art dexterity, and language skills such as talking, reading and writing. Children will become a part of a healthy atmosphere for learning if they are permitted to make choices based upon their interests and abilities.

Children will base their choices upon a number of criteria. They may select a particular activity because they want to be with a friend, or because they want to be with the teacher who is responsible for that activity. However, the prime consideration in most choices will be the interest in the activity, the skill to work with it, and finding success. The process of making a choice is a valuable learning experience for children. Making the decision itself is really not very difficult. The difficulty enters into the process when he must stay with a choice and accept the consequences of that choice. Giving him many threat-free opportunities to make choices can help the child develop the ability and self-confidence he needs to make decisions throughout his life.

Some learning enablers feel that they should plan all the activities for the child. Others feel that children should have part in planning the activities. If the teachers decide to preplan the activities, it is important that the planning be done with the child in mind. The relationship of the activity to the concepts being learned must also be considered. We cannot justify painting just for the experience of painting. We cannot plan to taste just because the children will enjoy the experience. The total teaching/learning plan must be considered. If the decision is made to include the children in the planning phase of the activity, teachers must be careful to do enough preplanning so that materials and equipment will be accessible to the children. If children are asked to help with the planning, their ideas and choices must be accepted by the teachers. A wise teacher will not defeat the purpose of pupil-teacher cooperation by deciding ahead of time the outcome of the planning session.

We must not fail to consider another important phase in the planning of learning activities. We fall short of our goals for learning once again, if the activities do not lead to application in the daily lives of the pupils. Activities must help the child become acquainted with God's Word and then integrate God's Word into his life.

The remaining chapters of Part III will be devoted to a wide variety of learning experiences which are appropriate for use in children's departments of the church.

With the listing or description of the activity, there will appear a code which will assist you in making appropriate choices. Following the name of each activity you will find numerals 1, 2, 3, 4, 5, 6, indicating appropriateness for grade level. *S* will indicate appropriateness for *small* group activity and *L* will indicate appropriateness for *large* group activity. In some cases both *S* and *L* will appear. This would indicate that the activity can be used in both small and large groups. The first letter will indicate preference. Large group will mean the total department group not to exceed 25-30.* Small group will mean that portion of the department group after it has been divided into class sections. The size should not exceed 5-7. The numbers given will change to correlate with the organization and size of your teaching units.

Each area will also include some information on materials that will be needed, the organization of materials, and a plan for the usage of the materials. Be ready to explore with fascination the world of activity!

CHECK TASK—*Refer to your "children's profile" notebook. Compare the needs of children and the activities that may be used to meet that need. List the activities which you used in a Bible learning situation. Discover others that would have been effective in that situation. Determine to use one new kind of activity when you work with a Sunday school class again. Plan now for that specific activity.*

*If the total department group exceeds 30 pupils, perhaps the group could be divided in half or a new department formed.

CHAPTER NINE

RESEARCH CAN BE EXCITING!

OBJECTIVE—*to explore a variety of research activities which will help the child to gather information and build concepts.*

Research. What a dull-sounding word! We often think of research as the scholarly pursuit of information gained by going through volumes of books difficult to understand. But research can really be an avenue of enthusiastic learning. Let's think of research as the gathering of information obtained through a wide variety of methods. Consider some exciting ways of working through research activities. Research activities will be made up of three very important elements:

Exploration
Investigation
Reporting or sharing information

Learners will need to have a reason for engaging in research activities. They will want to determine what information is needed and the best possible way of obtaining that information.

Field Trips: (1, 2, 3, 4, 5, 6; S L) Children can gain firsthand information when they leave the classroom and visit an area related to the study topic. Field trips need to be carefully planned. Begin by planning the trip with the children. Be sure the children understand the purpose of the trip and how it relates to their unit of study. Make necessary arrangements for the trip. Make an appointment. Arrange for adequate transportation. Field trip activities provide an excellent opportunity to involve parents and other interested adults as they are able to assist in the supervision of the trip. This activity may take place during the Sunday school hour or during the week. It will contribute much to the success of an exciting summer program when the time with the children may be increased. Field trips also provide a fine opportunity for the teacher and learners to become better acquainted.

The size of the group will need to be based upon the place to be visited and the transportation that can be provided. Rather than taking the entire group at one time, you may want to make several trips with smaller groups of pupils. A formal report of the trip is not necessary. However, the learners will want to talk about their trip and the information gained. They may even want to evaluate the trip as a learning experience. There will probably be some carry-over from the trip to other related activities within the classroom. Children may wish to share information by taking pictures or slides during the trip. It will be possible to share information through art activities, such as drawing or painting. Some trips may lead to dramatization.

Interviewing a Resource Person: (3, 4, 5, 6; S) Asking questions of another person is such a comfortable action for children that we need to be aware of ways to use this skill in learning activities. We may provide opportunities for children to interview the minister, a visiting missionary, other church staff members, and members of the community. Children will need assistance in planning an interview session, and will need the following information before the time of their interview.

1 A list of questions to ask. This may be determined by the group. Questions will be based upon the information needed by the group at the time of the interview. The purpose of the interview will be established.

2 The interviewer will need to know something about the person that is to be interviewed. This will allow him to feel comfortable in the interview situation.

3 It will be important to make an appointment or plan with the person being interviewed so that the time and the place will be suitable for everyone involved.

4   An individual child or a small group of children may go to conduct the interview, or the person being interviewed may come to the class.

5   A way to share information with the total group needs to be planned before the time of the interview. If a tape recorder is available, the entire interview may be recorded and shared with the group. Some groups have chosen to make a poster to share the information. Still others have used oral discussion as a means of sharing. Children will choose a way that is meaningful to them.

Listening Centers: (1, 2, 3, 4, 5, 6; S) Listening centers provide opportunities for research through a wide variety of prepared materials. Children who do not wish to use reading skills or oral language skills to gain information are very successful when permitted to work in listening centers. The material presented at a listening center is limited only to the equipment that is available to you. If the small group is working in an area that is close to other working groups, it will be helpful to have headsets so that the sound will not be disruptive to their thinking. A variety of projectors are available at a wide price range. Which of these possibilities is available to you?

1   Filmstrip and record combination. Moody Press and others make available fine filmstrips and records of Bible lessons. Filmstrips and records which will reinforce the application of the Bible lesson are also available. Check the local Bible bookstores. Your school district may also make available this kind of material to you.

2   Split/35 filmstrip and record. The Split/35 filmstrip may be used on a Stori-Strip viewer or with a filmstrip projector that is equipped with an adaptor. Gospel Light Publications has split/35 filmstrips relating to God's creation, a well-done science series, Bible lands, and some Bible lessons.

3   Tape recorders. Cassette tape recorders are becoming more and more widely used as their versatility is demonstrated. They are small, extremely easy to use,

relatively inexpensive, and offer many opportunities for use by both learners and teachers. Learners may listen to material that is being shared by other learners. They may use the recorders to make Bible lessons available to absentee learners.

4   Phono-Viewer: General Electric has manufactured the Show-'N-Tell Phono-Viewer. It is built like a small television set, lightweight and easy to transport. It uses a record and split/35 filmstrip which has been encased in plastic. Many Bible lessons from both Old and New Testament have been prepared for use with the Phono-Viewer. Its operation is simple enough that a small group of children can operate it independently. It is an excellent tool for home visitation and has been well received by both learners and parents. Either the teacher or a small group of children can use this method to share the Bible lesson with an absentee child. The Phono-Viewer is not equipped with a connection for headsets. If it is to be used by several pupils within the total group, you need to be aware of the sound that will be present.

5   Records. Listening to records at a listening center with headsets can become an effective means of research. Children may be able to understand something about the hymns used in a worship service through such a listening experience. Children have heard about David playing his harp. Think how this experience might become more meaningful as they listen to the music of a harp in a listening center activity.

When using listening center activities, it is important for the teacher to be aware of the information that is to be gained from the listening experience. Materials used need to be previewed by the teacher before they are used by the children. This is a good use of teacher planning time.

Moving Pictures: (1, 2, 3, 4, 5, 6; L and S) An increasing number of moving pictures are available for use by children who are working on research activities. Purchase of moving pictures is prohibitive in most situations. However, public libraries often make movies available, although not all are biblically correct. Teachers should preview them before class use. Many areas have a rental service for religious films. Watching a movie can become a valuable research activity when the researchers have been assigned to look for particular items. A chart or list of questions to be answered will be of help in guiding thinking and observing.

Books: (1, 2, 3, 4, 5, 6; S) The use of books as research materials is certainly not a new idea. Can you think of new ways to use books so that children will eagerly anticipate the opportunity of finding information in them? Too often books are placed on a table or a book rack and children are given little or no guidance in their use. The end result is usually no interest or use of the books at all. At best, the learner may look through the books very quickly and gain little information. The books chosen must be within the reading ability of the children who are to use them. If your church has a library, small groups of children, along with their leaders, need to spend some time there. These visits can result in an increased interest in library use and in the compiling of new information.

Books may be chosen at a "Book Center" that relates directly to the Bible lesson and to the application of that lesson in daily living. Places to locate information in the books may be pre-marked with cards that have questions on them. The learner may determine the answer and write it on the card. Children need to know that they can learn from pictures or charts, as well as from the words in the book. Books may be combined with listening center activities. The teacher or older learner may record the book on a tape. Small groups within the children's departments will find success in research as they listen to the recording and follow along in the book.

Some teachers have made game boards to accompany books used for research. The game board may include spaces for moving a marker as certain questions are answered in the book or as a given list of words is found.

It is important for children to become acquainted with the use of Bible dictionaries, commentaries, and the concordance. Two dictionaries which are helpful to children are these:

1   *A Bible Dictionary for Young Readers,* William N.

McElrath, Broadman Press, Nashville, Tennessee, 1965 ($2.95).

2 *A Picture Dictionary of the Bible,* Ruth P. Tubby, Abingdon Press, New York, 1949 ($2.00).

Children will benefit from making their own Bible dictionary. Use a large chart tablet and list Bible words as they are used in the Bible lessons. Children may illustrate the words by drawing appropriate pictures or by cutting them from magazines or books and pasting them in the correct places. This activity will permit the children to create a resource book that will have real meaning for them because of their involvement in its production. Fourth, fifth and sixth graders may wish to make their own individual Bible dictionaries. Provide composition books or notebooks. Have the dictionaries on hand at all times so that learners may add to them or refer to them for information when they need it. Dictionaries at this level may be illustrated with pictures or written definitions. This should be decided by the learner. There is very little value to a large group of dictionaries that have been completed in exactly the same way. The real learning occurs when the learner selects the words or phrases to be included and then further decides upon the way to include them.

Questioning: (1, 2, 3, 4, 5, 6; S and L) As a child feels a need for information, his first response is to ask a question. On the surface, this does not appear to permit much variety or creativity. Think about these ways of questioning. You will be able to add to the list as you work with the idea of research through questioning.

1 Informational Questions — These involve the discovery of facts. They are based upon what, who, when, why and how.

2 Provocative Questions — Those questions which may bring about different responses may be classified as provocative questions. It is a question that requires thinking and reaction on the part of the learners. It has no one correct factual answer.

3 Open-End Questions — Open-end questions may have more than one answer. The value of open-end questions lies in the necessity of considering more than

one point of view. Even after the discussion, there will be no conclusive answer. This kind of questioning will lead the learners to feel the complexities which are present in most life situations. If we are going to encourage multiplicity of answers and conclusions, we must be willing to give the learner time to think. We often admonish children to "think," and then demand an immediate answer.

In order for questioning research to be of real value, the child must be guided to consider several possibilities. He must learn to cope with the idea that often there are no absolute answers. The ability to accept variance in answers to questions will be an important step toward the acceptance of peer group and self even when opinions and beliefs differ.

Look and Listen Teams: (4, 5, 6; S) Two learners may decide to work together to look and listen for information, answers, and new material about a given subject. Teamwork is an important application of the teaching's of God's Word. This research technique will help put into practice the concept of acceptance of one another and of working together with a common goal. It will be important for the team members to agree upon the information that is being sought, the materials that will be used, and ways of reporting to a larger group, if appropriate.

Bible Reading: (1, 2, 3, 4, 5, 6; S) For years, Bible reading has been considered too difficult for children. We have read passages of the Bible to children, but they have done very little Bible reading themselves. Even the first grader, who is just beginning to unlock the communication process called reading, is thrilled to find that he can read an occasional word from the Bible. As reading skill is increased, more independent work in Bible reading may be accomplished. Let's think of some creative ways to encourage meaningful Bible reading.

1   Be sure that your own Bible reading has meaning. Do you read words only? Or do you read ideas and concepts? Having read them, do you practice them in daily living?

2 Help learners to understand the words that they are reading. This is a difficult task if we do not read for understanding ourselves.

3 Use several Bible translations to aid in finding the meaning of the passages being read.

4 Use a Bible dictionary. Encourage learners to make their own dictionaries.

5 Use clues, as in riddles, to encourage learners to find a specific verse.

6 Show a series of pictures. Read a Bible verse or short passage of Scripture. Match the verse with the correct picture.

7 Help learners become well acquainted with their Bibles through use of Bible games and Bible drills. These are often suggested in the teacher's book. Games and drills need to be free of competition, the reward being the increased effective use of the Bible.

8 Decide upon ways to use a Bible verse during the week. Be ready to report on the success of application to daily living the following week.

9 Even first grade learners will benefit from finding a given word in some portion of the Bible. For example, mark Genesis 37:1-5 in Bibles. Select words from the passage and write each word chosen on a separate word card. Permit the child to look in the marked portion of the Bible for the word on his card. You will be pleased with the interest and enthusiastic response that is evident throughout an activity such as this. The passage selected must be related to the Bible lesson. In Genesis 37:1-5, you might encourage the child to find *Jacob, Joseph, father, coat, son* and *loved.* Children may choose to add some of the Bible words to the Bible dictionary.

10 Learners at the fourth, fifth and sixth grade levels who read well can record at a listening center. If the tape recorder is portable, these recordings may be used by teachers and learners when visiting absentee pupils. Since the Bible is the very basis of all Christian education, it should be used with all learning activities. It must not be used with research activities only.

11 Use Bible reading to help with a contact during the week. A phone call or letter asking a pupil to be

ready to read some portion of the Bible on the following Sunday morning will be received with enthusiasm.

12 Choral reading of the Bible is often considered an oral expression activity. It is that. However, it becomes a part of research as the meaning of the passage is emphasized. We do not need to be concerned with rhythm, voice quality, or drama. Oral reading of the Bible will help bring about greater understanding. Reading as a group will make it possible for children who lack reading skills to participate, or to benefit from listening.

As you plan for learning experiences to accompany your next teaching unit, check these suggested research activities. Which ones are appropriate for this unit? Which ones provide experiences that will meet the needs of your group of children? How can you bring together space and materials so that they may be used effectively in research? How will your children feel about becoming involved in research activities?

When these questions have been answered, you are ready to proceed and schedule research as part of your Sunday plan.

CHECK TASK—*Using the information provided in chapter 9, and any other sources which are available to you, plan specifically for a research activity during your Sunday school hour. Gather the materials that will be needed. Consider ways to encourage research during the week at home. Plan for a worksheet which involves some research skills. Introduce and begin the work during the Sunday school hour. Encourage completion at home. In addition to reading the paper and pencil research, plan for a field trip or other research involvement activity.*

CHAPTER TEN

MAKE CONTACT WITH AN IMPACT: CREATIVE COMMUNICATION

OBJECTIVE—*to understand the several facets of communication; to provide opportunity for spiritual growth through the use of language activities. To assist the learning enabler in the task of learning to listen more and talk less.*

We often feel that in order for children to learn they must be quiet and listen. Research has shown us that the most effective learning occurs when the child is an active participant in the learning activity. Conversation, discussion, and many other forms or oral communication can be adapted to Bible learning activities.

Oral Language: Oral participation can involve the learner in many interesting and helpful learning experiences. Very young children will become a part of the Bible lesson as they help with the sound effects. As children become better acquainted with words and their meaning, they begin to feel comfortable using language to question, discover, and communicate ideas and feelings.

Brainstorming: (4, 5, 6; S) Teachers are often amazed at the wisdom of children when they feel free to express themselves. Brainstorming provides for the sharing of a great number of ideas about a given subject, event or question. The most important factor which will insure the success of a brainstorming session is the acceptance of every idea that is expressed. Children often learn more rapidly from each other than they do from an adult. As they experience the sharing of ideas within the peer group, they will be stimulated to evaluate and consider a number of ideas related to the subject that is being discussed.

Buzz Groups: (4, 5, 6; S and L) The organization of buzz groups involves a large group which has been divided into smaller ones. A total department could be involved. Small groups of four to six learners are located at different spots in the room. Usually all groups are considering the same topic, and ideas are shared quickly and easily. Everyone is encouraged to participate. Acceptance of all ideas is assured. Everyone within the group does not need to agree, but acceptance of the expression of an idea is a must. Someone in each group is selected to be the recorder or reporter. Before the session ends, the small groups assemble and each reporter shares a summary of ideas from his group. Children will be interested to see both the similarity and the difference of ideas that come from the several groups.

Open-End Sentences and Questions: (4, 5, 6; S) The use of open-end sentences and questions offers children an opportunity to think through ways of applying Bible truths to daily living. We need to encourage this carry-over continuously. Answers to open-end questions may be written, shared orally, dramatized or drawn. These oral activities may involve a large group, but it is recommended that you use small groups so that all pupils may have ample opportunity for participation. If the group becomes too large, much valuable time is spent listening and waiting for turns.

Speaker and Discussion: (4, 5, 6; L and S) Research, interview, and discussion can all be combined at this point to encourage speaking and listening skills. A speaker may be invited to speak to your department, sharing information that is of interest to the children. They may respond during a question and discussion period following the presentation. Small group discussion will bring about greater participation and a more personalized learning experience. This activity provides an opportunity for a combination of methods.

Discussion: (1, 2, 3, 4, 5, 6; S) Careful planning and preparation is necessary if children are to learn through discussion. Discussion can be aimless talk that does not increase information or skills. It can create misconceptions unless the learning leader is able to guide the discussion without dominating it. These basic guidelines will assist the learning leader who is responsible for a discussion.

1   Participants will feel more at ease if the setting is informal. Chairs arranged in a circle or semicircle will set the scene for an effective discussion.

2   The leader or guide needs to sit in the circle and become a part of the group.

3   All ideas that are contributed must be accepted with respect.

4   Avoid directing a specific question to any one child. Encourage participation of children as they feel comfortable and want to make a contribution.

5   Carefully help those who dominate a discussion to permit others to participate. You might say something like, "We like your good ideas, Tom. Now perhaps you would like to know what _____ thinks about it."

6   Avoid determining the direction of the discussion.

7   At the end of a discussion period, synthesize ideas if a summary is agreed upon. This does not mean that everyone agrees with all the ideas. The summary merely represents a pulling together of the many ideas that have been offered.

8   Record key ideas on charts for easy reference.

9   After the viewing of a film or filmstrip, a follow-up discussion will help summarize and share information.

Panel Discussion: (4, 5, 6; S and L) A small group participates while the larger group listens to the discussion and then reacts to it. Group members may respond with questions, statements of agreement, or a summarization. The small group in the panel discussion is usually aware of its participation ahead of time, so they can gather together and organize some information. Panel members use their research skills to locate facts.

Following the viewing of a film or filmstrip discussion will help children pull together ideas, feelings and facts that have developed as a result of exposure to the visual material. Children's reactions to films and filmstrip presentations will help the learning leader to know some of their needs.

Storytelling: (1, 2, 3, 4, 5, 6; S or L) Children are eager participants in a storytelling experience. The older pupil not only benefits spiritually when preparing a Bible story, but is well received when he presents it to the preschool or first and second grade classes. Storytelling for younger classes may be combined with an art activity as children prepare puppets, illustrations, or other visual aids to help tell the story. If it is not possible for your children to tell stories to other classes, consider the possibility of allowing them to record the stories with a tape recorder. Then the tape recorder could be used at a listening center in another class, or taken to the home of absentees.

Sharing: (1, 2, 3, 4, 5, 6; S and L) Sharing of ideas and information has been discussed in relationship to several other activities. We need to emphasize that sharing ideas orally is a very important phase of the Christian's life. Even a young child may become accustomed to telling others in his family or some of his friends about the love of God as it is revealed to us in the Bible. Gaining information is not complete until it is shared with another. Facts, as well as the warmth of a caring Christian, need to be shared. Words as well as feelings will help communicate ideas and concerns of one person for another.

Interview a Bible Character: (4, 5, 6; S and L) Have you searched for more creative ways of summarizing a study of a portion of Scripture that involves something more than a question and answer period? A planned interview with a "Bible character" can clarify concepts of the study in an interesting way. The interview itself will involve a small group of learners. However, the larger group may participate first as observers and then as questioners after the presentation.

If your Bible study has been involved with a Bible personality, permit someone in your group to take the part of that character. Another child or small group of children may plan the interview. As the Bible character is questioned, all in the group will pull together the information that is being shared. The interview may be recorded so that it may be used again at a later time. Costumes may be added to help set the scene for the interview. The total group may become involved as they listen and then present some additional questions, or talk freely with the Bible character.

This interview may take the format of the TV program, "This Is Your Life," or it may be related to written language activities if it is written and then included as a part of a newspaper-printing project. In any case, interviewing a Bible character is an interesting and enjoyable way for children to put together facts they have gathered about a person who is described to us in the Bible.

Bible Reading: (1, 2, 3, 4, 5, 6; S and L) Bible reading is just as effective in creative language as it is in research. Consider carefully the reading skills that have been developed by the learners before you ask them to participate in oral Bible reading. Children who feel secure and successful with their oral reading skills will volunteer to read orally with or for a group. Others will hesitate. The hesitant oral readers should not be forced to read orally when it is a difficult task for them, but should be given other choices which will mean success for them. The teacher will need to know well the abilities and skills of the learners in the group!

Once again, the children may respond when allowed to use the tape recorder for Bible reading. This will enable the less able readers to listen to a portion of the Bible as they follow along visually.

In addition to the tape, we have discovered that children enjoy participation in unison reading, whether the group be large or small. Passages of Scripture may be read responsively, in a choral reading situation, or as part of a dramatization.

The Bible needs to be read by teacher and learner, both individually and together, as some part of every Bible learning activity. If the learning project does not include the Bible in its planning and work, it becomes much the same as any project carried out by any group or organization. The inclusion of the Bible in the activity makes it one which can be used by the teaching program of the church. Activity without the Bible cannot be justified for use at church.

Conversation: (1, 2, 3, 4, 5, 6; S) Children very often feel a need to talk with a teacher. The teacher can be the caring adult that is needed at a given moment to really *listen* to the thoughts, ideas and feelings of the child. The conversation does not need to be directed or guided by the teacher. The child is the element in the conversation that makes it a valuable experience. His leading should be followed. Too often, teachers are concerned with transmitting facts and information. Be sensitive to the feelings and needs of children in your group. When the time is needed by a child for conversation, have the time available for unhurried, concentrated listening. The kind of conversation that will truly meet the needs of the child should involve a very small group, or perhaps only an individual child. It will be necessary to have an adequate number of staff members so that a teacher can be free from other responsibility for the time that is needed to give unhurried listening to a child's conversation. It is a good practice to have an additional "floating" teacher working in the department at all times. This person will be able to enter into meaningful conversation with children as needed and can also be available to assist in any of the Bible learning activities when a few moments of additional help are needed. This person should not be used as a substitute teacher. The responsibility of acting in the role of a substitute immediately takes away the freedom of time that is needed by that person to meet the unpredictable needs of the children.

Written Language: Participation in written language activities can provide valuable learning experiences for children when they are planned with the limitations of the children in mind, and when they provide no threat of failure. Many times children do not readily choose to participate in written activities because they seem too much like the schoolwork which may have produced feelings of failure and inadequacy.

Efforts in experiences involving written language should be accepted as they are made. Rigid criteria for judgment have no place in the learning program of the church. We are not concerned with perfect spelling, punctuation and sentence structure. More important is the sharing and expression of ideas that will help the learner make the information a part of his store of knowledge, ideas, and feelings.

Play, TV or Radio Script: (4, 5, 6; S and L) The written expression that is involved in the preparation of a play, TV or radio script can be related to dramatization as it is performed. The writing activity may involve a small group or sometimes an individual. The performance of the script will involve the total group as an audience, even though the actual performance will need a small group of learners.

Children are often able to express feelings as they arrange ideas in a sequence for performance. Oral expression, too, becomes more comfortable when you are involved with a script, costumes or puppets. You can see that many activities involve several kinds of media. It is not possible to completely separate an activity and classify it as having only one element.

Short Stories and Poetry: (1, 2, 3, 4, 5, 6; S) Even though a small group may be involved, the writing experience is an individual one as each child finds expression in writing a short story or a poem. First and second grade children will have great difficulty in writing ideas as quickly as they need to share them. The mechanics of writing may create a problem instead of providing a ready means of sharing ideas. The teacher or older child may assist by writing or typing the story or poem as the younger child dictates it to his own "secretary." This allows the story or poem to be recorded quickly and accurately without the painstaking motions of writing it on paper. Occasionally, older children will choose to use this technique of written expression.

The typewriter can be an aid to written expression. Older children may choose to use it independently. Younger children will be pleased with the experience of typing their own name after the teacher has recorded their ideas.

If first, second and third graders do wish to write their own ideas, provide materials that will make it easy for them to complete the taks. First grade children will use large size pencils easily. Writing paper used by local school districts will offer them a familiar format. First grade writing paper is usually composed of alternate lines, solid and slotted, with one-half inch space between them. A sample of the manuscript for easy reference should be available. You may wish to prepare such a sample on a large chart which may be posted in your "author's corner." Smaller individual samples for each child to refer to will help insure success. Second and third grade children still use paper lined in the same way, but the spaces between are usually smaller. Regular pencils may be used easily. Third graders will shift from manuscript writing to cursive writing about the middle of the school year. You will find that some third graders are very anxious for this shift and make the change quite easily. Others, who may not have fully developed coordination, will continue to use manuscript writing. The form of writing used is not important to the activity at church. We are concerned with the ideas and feelings that are expressed. Our concern is to provide the tools necessary to make the mechanics of writing simple and free of threat of failure.

Songwriting: (1, 2, 3, 4, 5, 6; S and L) Songwriting will be discussed more fully in the music chapter. However, writing words for songs may be considered a kind of written activity. Small groups of children are able to express ideas and feelings, and participate in a worship experience as they write words for a song. They may write words to a new tune, a familiar tune, or add verses to a known song. One group of children may write both the words and music to a song, or one group may prefer to write the words while another composes the melody. In this case the group must be small.

After the song is completed, it may be shared and learned by the entire group. This phase of the project will be more successful if the words have been recorded on a large chart. Illustrations will help younger children understand the words, while picture clues will help them learn it more easily. Your department may wish to write a number of songs and put them together in a book. The book may be duplicated and shared with other children's departments.

Diaries: (4, 5, 6; S) Writing diaries is really an individual project which may be shared by a small group. Each

MANUSCRIPT ALPHABET

Aa Bb Cc Dd Ee

Ff Gg Hh Ii Jj Kk

Ll Mm Nn Oo Pp

Qq Rr Ss Tt Uu

Vv Ww Xx Yy Zz

First Grade writing Paper Sample

Second and Third Grade Writing Paper Sample

child who is interested in keeping a diary will need to be provided with a composition book or small notebook. Recording daily events in their lives has always been a fascinating pastime for young people. As a child records the important events in his everyday experiences, he may be guided to apply the teachings of Scripture to his daily life. Sometimes the learner will not wish to share with the teacher some of the entries in his diary. If this happens, allow him his privacy to share only the items he does wish to reveal.

Writing a diary can be used to assist in the in-depth study of a Bible character. The learner will benefit from pretending to be someone that the Bible tells about. He may record actual events. This will provide an opportunity for the child to really know a Bible character. It will strengthen the concepts of sequence in Bible times. Additional learning will take place if the child is free to include suggestions of what his own actions might have been in the same situation. He should be encouraged to answer such questions as "What would you have done if you were Paul at the time of the shipwreck?" "How would you feel if you were put into prison, as Paul was?" Evaluation and application to daily living will occur as the learner thoroughly studies the life of a Bible person.

Newspaper Writing: (3, 4, 5, 6; S and L) Newspaper writing is really a small group activity that may be shared with the larger group upon completion. It may even be shared with other departments and with parents or other adults. The duplication and distribution of the finished product is important to the writers.

Sequence of events in Bible times, as well as understanding of the events, will come about as your pupils produce the "Jerusalem News" or "Antioch Times."

As you experience with your children the satisfactions of both oral and written language, you will be able to plan together many language activities. Children need to make contact with others. They have an urge to share experiences. They need to begin to experience participation in an audience situation. Courteous listening is developed through experience, not through talk and lecture. We live in a communication-oriented society. The church must have the ability to communicate something of God's Word to others. Expression through language helps to further the feeling of acceptance by the teacher and peer group. Language experiences have an important place in our plan for Bible learning activities for children's departments.

CHECK TASK—*Plan at least two creative language activities that you have not used before. Plan one to be an oral activity and the other to be a written activity.*

Make a tape recording of a small segment of the hour with your Sunday school class. It may be made during the small group time or during the large group time. Listen to the tape. Listen again and answer these questions about what you hear.

1 Who is doing more talking (teacher or student)?

2 Is the conversation question-and-answer (teacher or student)?

3 What percentage of the conversation is directed by the students, and what percentage by the teacher?

4 Is there a variety of methods obviously being used each Sunday?

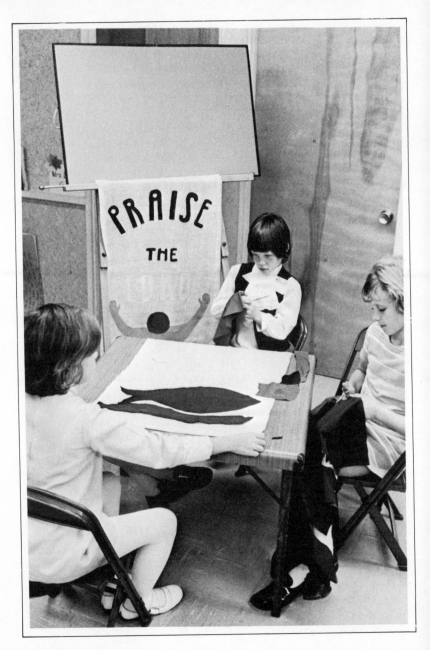

CHAPTER ELEVEN

CREATIVE ART: FUN WHILE WE LEARN!

OBJECTIVE—*to discover the possibilities of Bible learning and application of Bible concepts through the use of a variety of art activities.*

Creative art experiences provide an enjoyable way for children to learn Bible truths. The children's need to participate in active doing as they talk and listen, can help us utilize creative art activities.

As children plan and work through an art activity, they are able to put the events of a Bible lesson into sequence. Their manipulation of materials helps them to synthesize the Bible teaching. The greatest amount of learning takes place when the child is talking about the Bible truths as he works with the art media to express that truth. The learning enabler must be alert to the conversation and use of the Bible that occurs while the children are working. Art activities are usually most meaningful when a small group is participating, rather than the entire department.

Art activities make it possible for children to express ideas and feelings about the world around them. More than one sense can be utilized through art expression. Art permits the child to linger with a happy experience or to share an experience with others. Art can help him to organize ideas and feelings. Art can encourage sensitivity and self-confidence. The child who must cut out, color and assemble patterns made by others will become stifled and content to stop thinking. Following the exact idea of another takes very little thought.

We have considered the needs of the children in relation to art activities. Think about the end product. We are not really interested in the development of young artists! We are concerned with the learning experience of the children as they work through an art activity. Children not only become involved in the process of decision making, but learn to share and cooperate with their peers as well. They will have an opportunity for self-expression because they will "do it the way they want it to be." Art activities can truly be a meaningful way of learning Bible truths, and the relating of these truths to daily living.

Basic Supplies: Many satisfying art activities can occur with readily available and inexpensive materials. It would be impossible to compile a list of supplies that would be complete. Consider these items listed at random:

■ string ■ straws ■ soap ■ sponges ■ clothespins ■ newspapers ■ wax paper ■ paper plates ■ vegetables ■ wallpaper ■ sandpaper ■ paper bags ■ balloons ■ construction paper ■ paint ■ scrap lumber ■ nails ■ tools ■ sawdust ■ glue ■ crayons ■ chalk ■ buttermilk ■ magazines ■ boxes ■ egg cartons ■ wrapping paper ■ tissue paper ■ wooden picnic spoons ■ chenille wire ■ clay ■ playdough ■ salt ■ flour ■ cornstarch ■ food coloring ■ toothpicks ■ and so on.

Possibilities of materials for art activities are almost endless, and are limited only by the imagination of those involved.

Enlist the help of interested parents and church members in collecting usable items. Give them a list of articles that can be used. You will need to plan storage space for these materials. Classroom environment can be less effective if odds and ends of materials are stacked at random in every empty space. If shelves or cabinets are not available to you, perhaps you can obtain some see-through plastic sweater and/or shoe boxes for storage. These could be kept together neatly in an inconspicuous area.

The department should be equipped with paper of various sizes, colors and weights. Newsprint is a fine surface for drawing and painting. Local newspaper offices sell rolls of newsprint at a nominal cost. Often the roll-ends are free upon request. They simply need to be picked up and taken to the church. Wrapping paper or butcher paper provides an acceptable surface for finger painting, sponge painting and chalk work. Rolls of butcher paper are available in different sizes. The 36" width provides excellent material for murals and friezes. Construction paper should be available in assorted sizes and colors. A scrap box in which to store all of the odds and ends of paper will become a very important part of your supply area. Children will need different sizes and shapes of paper when you least expect that need to arise. A scrap box not only helps to meet this need, but can assist you in your thrifty use of supplies.

Your choice of materials for modeling will depend upon your group of children. Younger children will be content to use any of the soft doughs that are available. There are many recipes for making such doughs. Children will find that helping you make the dough is a valuable learning experience. These soft doughs are most satisfactory for children who have had little experience with clays. They will work well for modeling of objects and scenes that are temporary. The expense involved with soft doughs is nominal because they can be stored in airtight containers and be used again and again. Potter's clay is available in most areas at pottery factories or art stores. Older children may choose to use it, or they may feel that it is too childish for them. It will harden and become permanent if allowed to dry properly. It may be fired in a kiln, if one is available, and glazed or painted. Because of limited time, projects of this nature need to be part of a program that includes more than the Sunday morning hour.

Plaster of paris is probably the least satisfactory molding material for children. It dries and hardens so quickly that there is little opportunity for exploration and experimentation.

Supplies such as crayons, scissors, felt tip pens, brushes, paste, glue, pencils and cleanup materials should be readily accessible to the children. Once again, let us emphasize that your choice of materials will be based upon the children in your group and your teaching/learning situation. Recipes for your consideration will be found at the end of the chapter. Add those of your own that have proven useful.

Almost every teacher-training book includes art activities. You may see possibilities in some of the art projects that you observe in the school. Magazines that accompany church teaching materials include helps and ideas for art activities. You may want to begin a card file to help organize ideas for art activities. Looking through several books and magazines each time you want some help with an art project is too time-consuming. Plan for a file of 4" × 6" cards which will include the pertinent information about the activity. See diagram of card with suggested information.

Sample 4 x 6 file card for art activities file.

```
Name of Activity: _____

Materials Needed: _____
_____

Method: _____
_____
_____
_____
_____

Relationship to Bible Learning: _____
_____
_____
_____
_____
```

Now you are ready to go! Be ready to assist children in planning meaningful art activities with realistic goals. Children in small groups are capable of helping to work out the details of the art project. The learning enabler must be ready to help the group by: 1) knowing what materials are available or can be obtained, 2) knowing how much time and space will be required for the project, and 3) listing steps that the group plans to follow. Sometimes the preplanning of the teacher will be changed greatly as the group works together. It is important to be flexible even as the project is progressing so that changes can be made as they seem to be necessary to the child.

ART ACTIVITIES

As we think about specific art techniques, place them into the pattern of name, materials needed, method to be followed, and relationship to Bible learning. The suggestions given are only a few of the possibilities. It would not be possible to include every activity that may be used. Think of these as starters. Let your imagination move from each idea to as many adaptations as it can.

Tissue Paper and Starch or Shellac: (1, 2, 3, 4, 5, 6; S) Use white or colored tissue paper, a background piece of construction paper, starch or shellac, and brushes. Cut or tear tissue into a variety of shapes and sizes. Colored tissue may be "painted on" the background construction paper with starch or shellac. Starch is easier for young children to manage and clean up, but shellac will provide a more durable product. Overlap colors for interesting shades. Scenes from Bible lessons may be portrayed in this way. Stained-glass windows are quite effective. God's creation may be portrayed with cut-out shapes of tissue paper art arranged on a mobile or displayed in a window with light shining through.

String Painting: (3, 4, 5, 6; S) Use string, tempera paint, and drawing paper. Drop one end of the string into a container of paint. Pull the string up, squeezing out the excess paint between the sides of the container and a brush. Put the wet part of the string on the paper. Move it back and forth to leave a paint pattern. Or you may wish to lay a piece of construction paper flat on the table. Dip the string in paint, remove excess paint as before, place it in any shape on the paper. Place another piece of construction paper on the top and hold it in place with one hand. Pull the string sharply with the other hand, moving it in different directions as you pull it out. Repeat with different string and several colors. The resulting pattern may be used as a background area in a worship center, covers for song books, notebook covers, or framing for pictures.

Sand or Sawdust Painting: (3, 4, 5, 6; S) Materials needed are sand or sawdust, cardboard, tempera paint, paint containers, brushes, white glue or starch. Place a handful of sand or sawdust in a large container. Dip a wet brush into the dry tempera paint. With the wet brush stir the sand or sawdust until it soaks up the paint and becomes colored. Add more paint, if necessary, to color all of the sand or sawdust. Spread sand or sawdust out on newspaper to dry. (This preparation may be done during the week or on one Sunday to use the next. It will not dry sufficiently to use on the same day it is colored.) Plan the design or drawing on cardboard. You may sketch it lightly with pencil. Apply a thick layer of glue or starch to a portion of the design or picture. Sprinkle the dry, colored sand or sawdust over the glue area. Shake off the sawdust or sand that doesn't stick. Continue this procedure until the design or picture is complete. Children may choose to portray any portion of the Bible lesson. This technique is effective for map making. The sand painting may be used with a study of missions related to Indians.

Straw Painting: (1, 2, 3, 4; S) You will need to use paper or plastic drinking straws, a squeeze bottle with tempera paint and paper. Squeeze little pools of paint on a paper. Point the end of the straw in the direction you want the paint to move and BLOW! If young children are participating, you may wish to use food coloring in case the blowing becomes sucking. The straw should not touch the paint. A small amount of paint or food coloring is sufficient. As the child blows, the action may be related to God's wind action. You may wish to discuss the blending of colors in God's creation. The designs may be used as backing for paintings, parts of gifts for friends, or book covers.

Finger Painting: (1, 2, 3, 4, 5, 6; S) You will need paper with a smooth, shiny surface. Wrapping paper or shelf paper is satisfactory. There is a wide variety of "things" which may be used to finger "paint." Your purpose will determine which you select. Starch, with a sprinkling of dry powdered tempera, is quite satisfactory. You may wish to add such things as coffee grounds to brown paint if you plan to use the finger painting for the earth part of a mural. If the purpose of the finger painting activity is to help the children grow in appreciation of their sense of touch and taste as a part of God's creation, you may choose to use chocolate pudding, or Danish pudding, as the media. Older children will be able to use a number of colors in their finger paintings and thus create realistic scenes of a Bible story.

The area in the room where the children will paint should be covered carefully. The children, too, will need to be covered with old paint shirts or paint aprons. Water and sponges need to be nearby for cleanup which will follow the activity. Finger painting will not usually dry in one hour on Sunday. It will need to be completed on the Sunday before you wish to use it in a mural or frieze, if that is its purpose. If the completed project is to be taken home by the child, it will need to be left until the following week. Understanding of this before the child begins will help to avoid disappointment at the end of the hour.

Spatter Painting: (1, 2, 3, 4, 5, 6; S) Use an old toothbrush, vegetable brush, or window cleaner spray bottle, paper, scissors, thin tempera paint, or shoe polish. Fill the container with thin paint or shoe polish. Cover the work area with newspapers and place on them the paper to be spattered. Arrange leaves, grasses, other items, or designs and shapes which have been cut out, on the paper. Pin them lightly in place. Hold the spray container a short distance from the objects and spatter the paint. When you remove the items you will see that their soft outline remains. Objects may be rearranged and sprayed with another color. If you have a simple wooden frame with screen wire fastened on top, you can achieve the same results by dipping an old toothbrush into the tempera and stroking the wire. The relationship of the finished product to Bible learning is dependent upon the items chosen to be sprayed. Items of nature will help to reinforce teaching about God's marvelous creation. Designs and objects may be cut out to portray a Bible lesson or its application.

Soap Painting: (1, 2, 3, 4, 5, 6; S) With a rotary beater, beat two cups of Ivory Flakes and three-fourths cup water until the mixture is thick and creamy. Color it with food coloring, dry powdered tempera, or bluing. The soap paint may be spread with palette sticks or Q-Tips. It may also be used with hands. Soap paint adds texture to a crayon drawing of a Bible lesson. It becomes a stormy sea or a cloudy sky.

Drawing: (1, 2, 3, 4, 5, 6; S) Drawing may be accomplished with a variety of materials. Use any kind of paper that is available to you. Washable felt tip pens, paints, watercolors, pencils, and crayons all lend themselves to drawing. The child may decide on a picture or a series of pictures to portray a Bible story. The drawing may even pose a problem to be solved during discussion time. It may be quite detailed or simply portray stick figures, depending upon the skill and development of the child who is involved in the project. A series of pictures may be put together to form a time line, a mural, a movie, or a background for a puppet play. Drawings may be made to illustrate Bible verses. These drawings and Bible verses may be matched later in a game situation. The learning enabler needs to be cautioned when using drawing activities. Some children feel very inadequate when drawing, so another choice of activity must be available. Drawing is a comparatively simple activity to plan and organize. Let's not fall back on it too often because of its simplicity. Even an activity that is meaningful to learners will become boring and uninteresting when it is used too often.

Easel Painting: (1, 2, 3; S) Use newsprint or other paper of your choice, powdered tempera that has been mixed, brushes, easels, and cover-up aprons (#7). Mix the paint, using part water and part starch or liquid detergent. The addition of starch or detergent not only gives a pleasing texture to the paint, but makes cleanup easier. Easels may be the commercial floor type if they are available, or you may make a table or floor easel with pegboard as described in the chapter on equipment. Children will paint pictures of Bible stories, application of these stories, and pictures of their ideas about

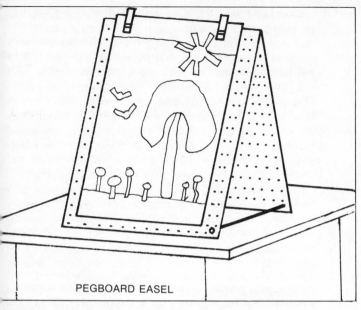

PEGBOARD EASEL

God's creation. Once again, the child needs to know that the finished product will need to dry thoroughly before it can be taken home.

Modeling: (1, 2, 3, 4, 5, 6; S) You will need to cover carefully the table or other work area, floor, and learners before beginning a modeling project. The choice of modeling material will depend upon your purpose. You may use any of several nonhardening dough mixtures which are included in the recipe section, if the object being made is temporary. If the finished article is to be permanent, you will need to choose a clay that will harden. Directions for drying are given with self-hardening clay. If the clay project cannot be completed on one Sunday, arrangements will need to be made to keep the clay soft for another week. Children may make objects to be used in Bible scenes or dioramas, such as dishes and lamps used in Bible times. They may wish to make clay tablets with some of the writings in Hebrew on them. Gifts of many kinds may be made for others. The child will benefit from his involvement in deciding which item to make.

Mural or Frieze: (1, 2, 3, 4, 5, 6; S) You will need to provide a large piece of wrapping or butcher paper. The size may vary although most groups can work well with an area of about three feet by six or eight feet. Size will be determined by your group, the work area, and the Bible concepts that will be included in the mural. Murals may be made in many ways. The decision process is a time of learning for the children. The group may decide to use tempera paint and brushes for the entire project, or they may decide to sponge paint the background and cut out or tear the articles needed for the scenes. The entire mural may be made by using torn or cut paper pasted in place. Finger painting may also be used for the background area. Articles cut out may be placed on a wet paint background and will remain firm without the use of glue. The possibilities for murals are limited only by the imagination of the group. With its utilization of Scripture and proper sequence of events, a mural or frieze can help synthesize the concepts about a Bible lesson and its application.

Sponge Painting: (1, 2, 3, 4, 5, 6; S) Materials needed are sponges (cut into rectangular shapes of about one-inch square and three to four inches in height) and clothespins. For use in painting activity, a clothespin is attached to one end of each piece of sponge. The sponge is dipped gently into a shallow container of tempera paint that has been mixed with starch or liquid detergent. The paint should be the consistency of a thick white sauce or gravy. The sponge is dipped into the paint and tapped onto the paper to achieve the desired effect. Sponge painting produces marvelous airy backgrounds of sky, grass, and earth. Springtime pictures can be very effective. Blossoming trees seem to leap from the paper when they have been made with sponge painting. Cleaning up after a sponge painting activity is relatively simple. The sponges clean easily, seldom is paint dripped on surrounding areas, and the painter usually has only to wash hands to be clean again. This is an excellent activity because children are provided with opportunity to plan, work with a group and make decisions.

Gadget or Vegetable Painting: (1, 2, 3, 4, 5, 6; S) You

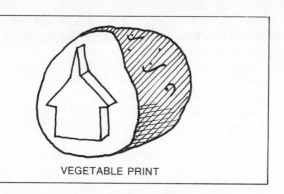

VEGETABLE PRINT

will need gadgets, such as cookie cutters, potato mashers, spools, cork and vegetables such as potatoes or carrots. The vegetables may be cut in half and then the stamp design cut on them. First and second grade children will need help in cutting the designs into the vegetables. The gadgets or vegetable designs may be dipped into a shallow container of thick tempera paint and then stamped on the paper. The choice of paper will depend upon its use. Wrapping or butcher paper may be used if the finished product is to be a gift wrap. Stamp designs of church symbols may be made on paper or muslin and used for a wall hanging in the worship center. One teacher used a set of Christmas cookie cutters to gadget paint the story of the birth of Jesus.

Dry Tempera Painting: (1, 2, 3; S) You will need to use dry wads of cotton and dry tempera. Wrapping, butcher or shelf paper will work well with this technique. Simply dip the paper into a container of water. When it is thoroughly dampened, place it on the table or other working surface. Dip the wads of dry cotton into the tempera which has been placed in shallow containers and apply the cotton to the paper. The result will be much the same as if the paper were dry and the paint mixed with liquid.

Repeat or Reverse Painting: (1, 2, 3, 4, 5, 6; S) The group will need to brush paint or finger paint on a tabletop. A top made of Formica or similar hard surface is desirable. When the painting is completed, place a piece of paper on the wet surface over the painting. Remove paper and allow to dry. Sponge clean area.

Picture may illustrate a Bible lesson or its application. It may be used for a puppet play background or as part of a movie box.

Crayon Resist: (1, 2, 3, 4, 5, 6; S) With crayons, make a design or picture of the Bible lesson on drawing or construction paper. Paint over the entire paper with watercolor or thin tempera. The paint wash will not cover the wax crayon. Children using a blue wash have made very effective pictures of God's creation in the sea. Stained-glass windows for the worship center have been made. A realistic storm may be created with crayon resist.

Paint and Wax Resist: (3, 4, 5, 6; S) Use wax paper, white paper, tempera or watercolor, and brush. Place the wax paper over a white piece of paper and draw on it with a pencil, being sure to press hard enough to transfer the wax from the wax paper to the white paper. Brush the paint over the wax lines on the white paper and watch the design or picture appear. Children enjoy using this technique to make a surprise picture of the Bible lesson to share with a friend.

Melted Crayons: (1, 2, 3, 4, 5, 6; S) Use your old crayon stubs for this one. Also use shelf paper, wax paper, a shaving tool such as a dull vegetable peeler, and some muffin pans. You may chip the crayons onto a piece of shelf paper. Place a second piece of paper on top of the sheet with the crayon chips. Use a warm iron to press on this second paper and melt the crayon. After you remove the top paper, you can draw with a black crayon over the melted colors or use your scissors to scratch a design or picture into the wax.

You may choose to sprinkle the shavings of wax crayon on a sheet of wax paper. Place a second sheet of wax paper over the shavings. Press the sheets together with a warm iron. If you wish to use this art piece to mount Bible pictures or verses, place them between the sheets of wax paper before the second wax paper sheet is added and the two pressed together. The wax will secure the pieces of wax paper together with the Bible verses and/or pictures firmly between. This will result in an attractive gift for a shut-in, friend, or an attractive wall hanging for the worship center.

If you want the crayons to melt and flow together smoothly, iron back and forth. If you desire a spotty effect with brilliant colors that do not flow together, lift the iron as you move it from place to place over the paper. The iron only needs to be warm, so children can use it with safety. It need not be heated so that it will be hot enough to burn.

Stub-ends of crayons may be used in still another way. Melt the stub-ends in muffin pans over very low heat (a candle will supply enough heat). Be sure to line the muffin pans with cupcake papers for ease in cleanup. Dip a Q-Tip or Popsicle stick into melted crayons and drop or brush onto textured rough paper. If the melted crayons are permitted to harden in the muffin pans, the paper can be easily peeled off and they will be fine gifts for the early childhood classes. The resulting size, shape and texture of the crayon will be very pleasing for the younger children. Even first and second graders will enjoy the novelty of such a crayon.

Chalk Drawing: (1, 2, 3, 4, 5, 6; S) Chalk, newsprint, butcher paper, construction or drawing paper, and hair spray serve as basic materials for chalk drawing. Use chalk very much as you would crayons to make a Bible story picture, mural, or design. Chalk colors may be mixed with tissue or fingers. Spray the finished picture with hair spray. The spray will act as a fixative and the chalk will not rub off.

Chalk and Buttermilk: (1, 2, 3, 4; S) Cover work area and surrounding surfaces with newspaper. Gather your materials of drawing paper or construction paper, buttermilk, chalk and hair spray. Cover the drawing paper with buttermilk. You may do it with a brush or with fingers and hands as in finger painting. Use the chalk as crayons to complete picture or design. Some groups have enjoyed writing Bible verses with chalk on a buttermilk surface. Size of the paper will depend upon your purpose. The chalk on the buttermilk will produce more vivid colors than are usually achieved with chalk alone. Hair spray, together with the buttermilk, will set the chalk so that it will not rub off.

Collage: (1, 2, 3, 4, 5, 6; S) An experience with collage can reveal a limitless number of available materials.

Basically, it will require a firm base, white glue, or other strong fixative, and the materials that the group has chosen to use. The materials for the collage may include such items as beans, buttons, greeting cards, chenille wire, bits of string, thread, yarn, toothpicks, scrap paper, cork, plastic foam, styrofoam, feathers, cotton, straws, lace, fabrics, sandpaper, macaroni of many shapes, burlap, net, felt, ribbon, velvet and endless others. Here is another opportunity to involve parents and other church members in a "save material" project. You may decide that your classroom needs a "collage box." It will become a valuable source of materials. Not only will it be used for collage projects, but it just may supply the sequin or button that is needed to complete a puppet or the scrap material that is needed for a costume to aid in a dramatization.

Collage materials may be pasted or glued to paper or fabric. They may help the child to express a feeling or a concept about the Bible lesson. They should be put together with care to illustrate the Bible story.

Some of the most meaningful collages have been made in connection with a study of the creation of the world. Think for a moment about the endless possibilities for collage materials within the realm of nature. Seeds, shells, bark, leaves, dried twigs, grasses, pinecones, nuts and many other items may be put together to represent the wonders of God's creation.

Paper bag slide projector: (1, 2, 3, 4, 5, 6; S) A lunch-size paper bag can be used to advantage in many learning projects. The only materials needed are the paper bags, strips of paper, crayons, pencils and scissors.

Cut a large opening on one side of the bag. Clip off the base so that a drawing on a strip of paper cut to slide through can act as the filmstrip or slide. Let the learner discuss his own story as he holds the projector in front of the group. Or, several children may work on individual frames to tell the story and tape them together to make a complete story filmstrip. Children may alternate frames with problem situations and Bible verses to help solve the problems. The projector will then become an object to help stimulate discussion.

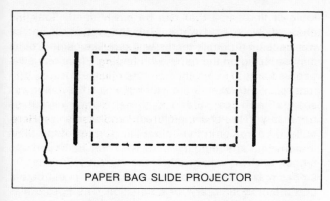

PAPER BAG SLIDE PROJECTOR

Crayon Rubbings: (1, 2, 3, 4, 5, 6, S) You will need to use two sheets of newsprint, construction or drawing paper, crayons and objects to be rubbed. Collect textured articles such as leaves, tree bark, screen, fish net, burlap, or torn or cut shapes which will tell a Bible story. Arrange the items on one sheet of paper. Place the second sheet on top. Rub over the entire surface with the broad side of a crayon. The finished paper will look something like a shadow picture. Children may wish to add a Bible verse, descriptive sentence or poem.

Crayon Etching: (4, 5, 6; S) You will need to have ready wax crayons, paint, white paper and a scratching tool (the edge of a spoon, scissors, or a nail). Cover the white paper with one or many crayon colors. Color heavily to leave a thick layer of crayon. Completely cover this with black crayon. Now scratch through the black with your tool. Another way to work with a scratch is to rub over the crayon colors with black or violet paint that has been mixed with a little liquid detergent. Now draw with the tools. Children will enjoy recording Bible verses or making plaques with the crayon etching technique.

Wet Chalk Paintings: (1, 2, 3, 4, 5, 6; S) Shelf paper, sticks of chalk, water and hair spray or sugar water will be needed for this activity. Also, the work area will need to be protected with newspapers or plastic covering. Old shirts or paint aprons will be needed to cover the children. Soak a piece of shelf paper in a sink, or sponge the paper with water. Smooth out the wet paper on a table or floor area that can be easily dried. Soak the chalk sticks in cold water. Rub the wet chalk on the wet paper. The chalk marks will look like paint. Colors may be mixed on the paper with fingers. Place on newspapers to dry. The finished picture may be sprayed with hair spray. However, if the water in which the paper was soaked had sugar added to it, hair spray will not be necessary. The chalk pictures may be displayed on bulletin boards or in the hallway to help tell of the Bible lessons that are being learned. They may be bound into a book to share with another department or friends. Or, stories may be added to their book which could be put into the church library for circulation. The possibilities for use are endless.

Tin Can Painting: (3, 4, 5, 6; S) Children need to use glue, string, felt scraps, yarn and a can from which both ends have been removed. Glue the string, yarn and felt scraps to the can to form a pleasing design or picture. Roll the can over a piece of cardboard or linoleum which has been covered with printer's ink, or a mixture of one teaspoon of vaseline and dry tempera paint. Roll the "inked" can over the paper for printing. Tin can painting can be a way to tell a Bible story; it can serve as wrapping paper for gifts, or it can be used as a wall hanging. Often a Bible verse can be added, and the hanging used in the worship center or as a point of beauty in a research center. It can be shared with other departments within the church.

Stitchery: (2, 3, 4, 5, 6; S) A loosely woven fabric, such as burlap, is a good material for stitchery experiences for children. In addition to the fabric, children will need yarn needles with large eyes and an assortment of yarn. Children will need to plan their picture, symbol, or Bible verse before they begin to work on the fabric. Encourage planning on paper and perhaps a sketch of the burlap. Children who are involved with stitchery for the first time may need some help in learning how to execute a number of kinds of stitches. Finished panels may be used for wall hangings, pillow tops, or they may be mounted on cardboard or chipboard and framed as a picture. They may be fringed and used for place mats. They may eventually be used for gifts. Some first grade children may be able to handle the yarn and needle and might be very interested in a stitchery project. However, as a general rule, second grade is soon enough to become involved in this activity.

Puppets: (1, 2, 3, 4, 5, 6; S) Making and using puppets provides a variety of rich learning experiences for the child. We will consider the making of puppets as an art activity and the using of puppets as a part of dramatization. It is difficult to separate the two elements. Children may also become involved in a written language experience as they plan and write the puppet script. At this point, let's consider the art activity that is taking place as the child makes a puppet to use. There are many kinds of puppets. The child will need to be involved in some decision making to determine the kind of puppet to make.

The materials needed will be listed briefly with each kind of puppet. The purpose of the puppets will be to express feelings, concepts and understanding of Bible lessons through dramatization.

a   Chenille wire puppets. Bend one chenille wire in half and insert into wooden bead head or small styrofoam ball. Add arms with another chenille wire. Twist to form body and legs. Make robe from cloth or crepe paper. Gather around waist with small piece of yarn or chenille wire. Draw face on head with crayons.

b   Wooden spoon puppets. Use the back of the bowl of the spoon for the face of the puppet. Yarn may be added for hair. Fabric or crepe paper gathered around the handle of the spoon becomes the clothing as well as the concealer for the hand.

c   Paper sack puppets. You may stuff the bag with shredded pieces of newspaper. Tie off the bottom of the bag and insert a dowel or a ruler to serve as a handle. Drape a piece of cloth over the stick. Make hair of yarn and draw or paste on the eyes, nose and mouth. Another kind of paper bag puppet may be made by leaving a new bag closed. Make the face on what would be the bottom of the bag if it were opened. Place the mouth so that the upper half is on this section and the lower half is on the side of the bag. Insert hand into the bag and move it to make the mouth look as if it is opening

CHENILLE
WIRE
PUPPET

WOODEN
SPOON
PUPPET

PAPER
BAG
PUPPET

HANGER
AND
NYLON
PUPPET

and closing. Yarn may be added for hair. Fabric or paper may be cut and added for the remaining features and clothing. Paper bag puppets may be people, Bible characters, animals, or just about anything the child imagines them to be. This is a very simple, inexpensive puppet to make.

d   Papier-mâché puppets: (3, 4, 5, 6; S) Younger children may wish to experiment with papier-mâché, but considering our limited time on Sunday and the skill and development of children, papier-mâché is not recommended for children younger than third grade. An exception to this recommendation would be groups of children who meet more often than once a week on Sunday or who meet for extended periods of time.

A very satisfactory base for a papier-mâché puppet head would be an oval-shaped balloon. Blow up the balloon to desired size. You may wish to cover the balloon with a light coating of salad oil. This will assure easy removal of balloon when the papier-mâché dries. Starch and paper towelling, or strips of newspapers make a satisfactory covering for the balloon. As each layer is added and allowed to dry, the form will become stronger. Spray starch and facial tissue may be used just as effectively as starch and paper towelling. A mixture of wheat paste may be used instead of starch, if desired. When all layers are completely dry and hard, pop and remove the balloon. If it has not been covered with salad oil, it may be more difficult to pull the balloon away from the papier-mâché covering. When the balloon has been removed, complete the puppet by painting it, adding hair, facial features and clothing.

e   Hanger and nylon face puppet. Bend a wire clothes hanger into a reasonably round or oval shape, like a face. The hook or handle of the hanger becomes the bottom of the puppet and is used by the child to hold the puppet. Stretch an old nylon stocking over the hanger and secure it at the top and bottom. The face may be made of cut or torn construction paper and glued to the nylon. Yarn may be sewn around the edge of the hanger for hair. Use fabric for clothing. It can be fastened about the hook and it will cover the hand as it is being held during the play.

f Life-size puppet. Draw around a child on cardboard and paint as desire If the puppet is to be flat and used with a stick, only one figure will need to be cut. If you wish to have dimension, cut two bodies, stuff with newspaper strips and staple together.

There are many more than six kinds of puppets, but these suggestions will help stimulate your imagination. As you plan and work with groups of children you will discover others that will be meaningful to your group.

CLEANUP TIME

Let's think for a few minutes about the cleanup period that inevitably accompanies an art experience. Preventive cleanup is the key to a happy experience. Of prime importance is the necessity to protect the clothing of children. Father's old shirt, put on backwards and buttoned, will cover almost all of a child. If you wish to make special paint aprons, patterns are available in sewing pattern books. Carefully covering the work area and the floor around it will prevent some scrubbing. Newspapers or newsprint may be rolled up and thrown away at the conclusion of the activity. If your classroom is equipped with a sink area, cleanup will be easier. Many classrooms are not equipped with sinks and the cost of remodeling to include one is prohibitive. A plastic pail, dishpan, or other suitable container with water, and a good supply of paper towels and sponges will do the job.

You have probably noticed that the art activities have been checked for small group participation. It is unrealistic to think that a group of more than five to seven children can participate in a given art experience with satisfactory results. The involvement with the large group occurs in the sharing experience.

We have not discussed such techniques as mosaics, blockprinting, blueprinting, wrinkle painting, chalk and carbon, and many others. It is impossible to present all of the possibilities for art activities in a book of this size. Your imagination will take over here. If you need further help, check the Bibliography for additional reference materials.

Finger Paint # 1, 2

1 cup soap flakes
2½ cups liquid starch
⅛ cup talcum powder

Beat with an egg beater. Divide into several containers and color with powdered tempera.

2 cups cold water
powder paint for coloring

12-oz. box of cold water starch
an equal amount of soap *flakes*

Mix the starch and soap flakes together. Add the water slowly while stirring. Beat the mixture until it reaches the consistency of whipped potatoes. Add tempera— dark colors will show up more effectively than light colors.

Magic Modeling Goop

1 cup table salt
⅔ cup water

1 cup cornstarch
½ cup cold water

Mix salt and ⅔ cup water in saucepan, stirring until mixture is well heated. Remove from heat and add cornstarch which has been mixed with ½ cup cold water. Stir quickly. Mixture should be consistency of stiff dough. If it does not thicken, place over low heat and stir about one minute. Color with food coloring or leave white and paint with tempera. Mixture will keep indefinitely in plastic bag. No refrigeration is necessary. Objects will dry at room temperature in about 36 hours. Large solid objects should be pierced to allow drying inside. A coat of shellac or clear spray will give a beautiful finish.

Cloud Dough

6 cups flour
1 cup salad oil
water
food coloring

To 6 cups flour and 1 cup salad oil, add enough water to make dough soft and pliable. Food coloring may be added to entire batch or to individual pieces as used. This dough is very soft and elastic. Keep in covered container or plastic bag.

Flour and Salt Clay

(enough for approximately 10 children)
6 cups flour   2 cups water
1¾ cups salt

Mix flour and salt together thoroughly, adding water slowly until it is dough. Knead on board—roll out and cut or shape as desired. Bake at 225 F. for one hour in a regular oven for a very hard product. Baking is not necessary. You can allow it to dry thoroughly. When finished, paint and shellac product. If item is to be hung, add a paper clip to back before drying as it can be used for a hanger when finished.

HOW ABOUT ADDING INTEREST TO YOUR DOUGH MIXTURES? In addition to the food coloring or tempera, add just a bit of flavoring. Orange dough with orange extract will appeal to the sense of smell because it will really smell like oranges. Cinnamon, lemon, strawberry, cherry, pineapple, almond, and others work well.

Crepe Paper Modeling Mixture

1 cup flour
1 tablespoon salt
1 package crepe paper
water

Cut the package of crepe paper into small bits. Place them in a mixing bowl and cover with water. Soak until soft, then drain off the excess water. Add salt to flour. Gradually add this mixture to the wet paper until it makes a thick dough. Knead until thoroughly blended.

Play Dough

(This dough will stay moist for a long time)

½ cup salt
1 cup flour
2 teaspoons cream of tartar
1 tablespoon cooking oil
1 teaspoon powdered alum (preservative)

After mixing the dry ingredients, add the liquids. Bring to a boil and cook 3 minutes. Drop on wax paper and knead as soon as it cools. Store in an airtight container.

CHECK TASK—*Select two art activities that are new to you, or that have not been used with your group of children. Plan to use these activities during the Sunday school hour. Gather the necessary materials and/or equipment. Prepare the area to be used and be certain that all materials are out and ready for use.*

CHAPTER TWELVE

LET'S BE DRAMATIC!

OBJECTIVE—to understand the relationship between dramatic experiences and Bible learning.

IN SOMEONE ELSE'S SHOES

Combine a child's imagination, feelings and actions in dramatic activities and the end result can be very meaningful. Drama provides a unique opportunity to experience the events in the life of another person. The marvelous imagination of a child allows him to feel as David did when he was playing his harp for the king. A six year old can identify with Joseph as he has difficulty with his brothers. He can feel the temporary hopelessness as he is put into the pit. This experience can remind him of times in his own life that required forgiveness in his relationships with brother or sister. The wonder of sharing a small lunch with Jesus and the amazement that God could multiply it for five thousand people are only a few of the feelings a child will experience through dramatic activities.

FEELING IS UNDERSTANDING

The action and adventure involved in so many of the Bible incidents make Bible lessons fine material for dramatic activities. Roleplaying and open-end action experiences help to relate the Bible truths to our own lives. Children can begin to really feel the words *love, share, kindness, friendliness, care, help,* and *obey*.

Let's think of creative dramatics as the acting out and

experiencing of a piece of fine literature. In the learning program of the church, it would provide an opportunity for children to "feel" characters from the Bible. An understanding of Bible lessons would be increased because of a feeling for the Bible characters. Creative dramatics does not mean that the children write their own play and then produce it. Creative dramatics must be accompanied by storytelling.

Why is it important to allow children to play a story? Playing a story is not a waste of time, done only for entertainment. Ideas, feelings, and concepts of the story they play can become part of the child. Children not only enjoy playing a story, but they begin to have an appreciation for other people who may be different from themselves. It helps them to stretch out to other people in other times and places. The Bible story comes alive in the minds of the children and helps them understand and accept the behavior of others.

INSIGHTS FOR THE TEACHER

Teachers, too, benefit from creative dramatics. It affords the teacher an opportunity to know the children better, and to become more keenly aware of their strengths and weaknesses. Undetected interests and needs may become evident through dramatic activities.

DRAMATIC ACTIVITIES

Playing a Story

The timing of "playing a story" is a critical factor in the success of the experience. The time to play a story is right after the story has been told. Children will need some guidance as they plan and prepare to play a story. The presentation may be very simple. If the interest of the group indicates that they wish to extend the experience, then add costumes, props and/or scenery. The play may be shared with the total department, with other departments, or even with parents. However, this is not necessary for the children to benefit and learn from the experience.

Guiding the playing of the story might include the following steps:

1   Tell the story to the group doing the dramatizing. Use conversation as well as description.

2   Review the story with the group. Guide them to think through the story and sequence of events by asking questions.

    a   What happened first in the story?

    b   Who were the people?

    c   What did they say?

    d   How do you think they felt?

    e   What happened next in the story?

3   Guide the group to identify the characters in the story. You may decide to list them on a chart.

4   Decide who will play each character. If there are several children who wish to play the same part, perhaps the story can be acted out more than once so that they may have a chance to be the character of their choice.

5   Discuss the scenes to be played in the story and the period of time each one covers.

6   Determine the areas for the action.

7   Act out the story without props and costumes. If a child pauses, ask a question to help him remember the action of the story.

8   Evaluate with the group the acting out of the story.

9   Discuss the scenery needed, if any. Make plans for this and decide who will make it.

10   Select costumes, using the dress-up box. Additional props and costumes may be prepared if needed.

11   Play the story using costumes and props.

12   Evaluate the story. Question and discuss.

Use your imagination to plan for materials that may be needed.[1] You may wish to use pictures to help clarify meaning or to provide information about background and costumes. Plan for an area in the room that can be cleared of furnishings and used as a stage for the dramatization.

Your dress-up box will provide another opportunity for the involvement of others. Many of the items in it can be collected from any number of people within your church membership. The contents of the box are limited only by your imagination. Elsie Rives and Margaret Sharp suggest a starting list in their book, *Guiding Children*.

1   Pieces of striped or solid materials in two-yard

lengths, folded with a neck area cut. These pieces will slip over the head easily and make authentic-looking biblical robes.

2   Scarves and sashes
3   Triangular pieces of materials for headdresses
4   Top of nylon stocking cut in bands or elastic bands to hold headdress on head
5   Beads and other costume jewelry
6   A mat, a crown, a shepherd's crook
7   A hat, a sombrero, an umbrella
8   Curios and dress from other lands
9   Sandals[2]

Pantomime

Dramatization may take on other forms. It need not be limited to playing a story. Pantomime is another often-used form of dramatization which will help make the Bible story a part of the pupil. Pantomime involves memory, emotion recall, story action and characterization. When the learner has worked his way through these areas and has presented his interpretation through pantomime, the Bible truth has truly become his. In addition to the pantomiming of a story, learners will sometimes choose to pantomime a Bible verse. This will help them put the Bible truths into their own lives. In order to pantomime the Bible verse "Love one another," the learner must think about ways to show love. When he has thought of ways and shared them with his group, he is more likely to carry them out during the week than if he had just repeated the words of the verse.

Many songs which children sing lend themselves to pantomime. Children may show through pantomime the way the music makes them feel. They may show the action of the song or the meaning of the song as they understand it.

Picture Posing

Picture posing may be considered a simple form of pantomime. It involves the learner as he pretends to be one of the characters in a picture, and can be done with or without costume. Young children can participate in this activity with success. Pictures chosen should be based upon the learning unit in progress. They may be biblical or modern-day pictures which are related to the unit. In order for children to benefit from picture posing, it must be preceded by a questioning, thinking discussion which includes something of the action in the picture, the feelings of the characters, and the predictable outcomes based upon these feelings. Sometimes the children may wish to include a narration. If the posing is to be presented to a larger group, that group may become involved and asked to reply to the pose with an appropriate song or Bible verse.

Tableau

The tableau may also be a form of pantomime which will involve a larger group of children. The action of the story, Bible verse or song, may be posed by a small group, but the larger group may be a part of the crowd included in the scene. At times, costumes may be used to add to the authenticity of the scene. Children may decide to include a narration, or to have one of the characters from the tableau step out, speak, and then return to the motionless pose.

All pantomime activities provide opportunities for the child who does not verbalize well to participate. Make a list of the Bible lessons, Bible verses and modern-day situations which lend themselves to pantomime. You may be surprised to note how many times this dramatic activity could be included in your plans for Bible learning activities.

DRAMATIC ACTIVITIES CAN INCLUDE CREATIVE WRITING

Think about relating some creative writing to dramatic activity. Some children may want to write a script for a stage play, a radio or TV play. Once again, the preparation will be completed with a small group and then shared with the large group. The scripts may involve Bible lessons, missionary stories or modern-day application stories. Plays and TV scripts may call for costumes, whereas a radio play would not. Interest and enthusiasm will be heightened with the inclusion of microphone, tape recorder, sound effects, and TV cameras.

Choral Speaking

Choral speaking involves a group of voices working together to interpret a passage of Scripture, poetry or prose. Children need to be well acquainted with the passage to be read. If possible, the passage used should be duplicated so that each pupil will have a copy. Or, you may wish to make a large chart to be posted in the classroom. Be certain that the meaning of the passage being read is clear. Choral reading should be an enjoyable experience. The goal is not perfection in your pupils' delivery, but an appreciation for the sounds and meanings of words as they are put together. The application of the passage to the lives of your pupils is of utmost importance.

The learners will benefit from working with the teacher by planning ways to divide the passage, by selecting which voices will speak which phrases, and by deciding how each part should be read.

Roleplaying

This activity is concerned with an entirely different kind of dramatic experience. It involves the learner in a drama which is filled with conflict or problems. It helps the learner identify with and understand the feelings of others. It helps to clarify concepts of "If I were that person, I would _____." When we have an opportunity to "put ourselves in someone else's shoes," our actions are not always so certain.

Roleplaying does not involve the use of costumes, props, scenery or practice. Real or imaginary situations may be used for roleplaying. However, if the experience is to have real meaning, the situation must be related to the unit being studied and the immediate life needs of the learners. Roleplaying is not easy for some children. Sometimes they will feel self-conscious and will not wish to participate. Encouragement should be given, but the child need not be forced to participate if he is not comfortable doing it.

The values of roleplaying are many. Children are able to feel positively about problem situations. They begin to realize that problems are a part of living and that they are not the only ones who may face them. They will also be helped to know that there may be many solutions to a given problem. It will be the responsibility of the group and the teachers to guide the thinking just enough to help children search for solutions built upon Christian principles.

Puppet Plays

What part do puppets have in dramatic learning experiences? Puppets help a child develop creativity. Storytelling and oral language experiences are enhanced by the use of puppets. Children who may have some difficulty in expressing their feelings will be better able to put feelings into words and actions if a simple puppet is involved. Puppet plays also strengthen listening abilities and teach peer group cooperation.

This activity may be written either by the teacher or pupils, and then dramatized with puppets. Or, puppets may be used in a spontaneous reaction play that does not have a set script. Both have value for children. Puppets may be used to dramatize Bible stories or to play out present-day situations. Let children decide the kinds of puppets they will use. Puppet making is an art activity in itself and was discussed in chapter 11.

Staging of the puppet play need not be elaborate. It is sufficient to use a box on a tabletop and a curtain stretched across the playing area. A folding screen may serve as a backdrop. A movie screen may be used and the puppets used in a shadow play behind it.

Encourage children to use puppets so they can learn to share information about Bible truths, demonstrate Bible truth applications and think through problem situations.

CHECK TASK—*Begin to collect items for a costume box. Have the box available in your classroom for use at appropriate times. Select puppets that you will be able to use with many Bible lessons. Make samples and provide opportunity for children to make others. Have puppets available for use.*

CHAPTER THIRTEEN

MAKING MELODY UNTO THE LORD

OBJECTIVE—*to become acquainted with a variety of possible musical experiences that may be used with children in the Sunday school.*

MUSIC A PART OF THE CHILD

Observe a child. Watch the way some form of music becomes evident in his activity. Humming, whistling, and singing short simple jingles, are natural ways for children to express themselves. Music seems to be interwoven into their very lives as they walk, jump, and even speak rhythmically.

This tells us, then, that children do not need to be equipped with special talents to enjoy participating in music learning activities. However, some children may hesitate to become involved in an activity related to music. The teacher needs to guide music experiences with patience and understanding. The invitation to participate must be sincere, accepting, without push or pressure.

Musical experiences may include singing, listening, writing, or instrumental and vocal activities. When children find success and enjoyment through musical experiences, they will probably return to the music center for further success and enjoyment.

MUSIC FOR DIFFERENT PURPOSES

Music experiences may be used with both small and large groups. While smaller groups may choose to work with music during the Bible learning activity period, the entire group may participate in singing during the departmental sharing time.

Creating readiness for worship   Music may set the scene and bring about readiness to listen to the Bible lesson, a missionary story, or special speaker. It may instill in the child a feeling of enjoyment and beauty as he sits in God's house. It may help the child grasp Bible truths, as well as ideas about the church, God and Jesus. Music may aid the child in expressing thanksgiving, love and praise to God. A very real worship experience may be initiated with music.

Developing listening skills   Listening is a skill that does not just happen. We must be ready to teach listening skills. The teacher must first listen to the music before it is used with the children. The equipment needs to be checked so that operating problems can be solved before the children become involved. If this has been done, then you are ready to introduce valuable listening experiences.

Listening values can be increased if the children are instructed to listen for particular items. You may ask them to identify a song or instrument. Listening to music to answer questions about feelings can be a helpful experience for children. Older children will be interested in comparing some hymns of the church today with some of the psalms and hymns in the Bible. They will discover similarities and differences. They might even like to try to compose tunes for some of the Bible psalms.

Children will enjoy listening to recorded music at a listening center. The music may be instrumental, or it may include the voices of children and/or adults. Children will find themselves singing along with the recording. Listening to music might also motivate a child to express his feelings through an art activity or drama.

Expressing feelings   After a time of listening, children will need to have an opportunity of sharing and participating together in some expression of their own. They may wish to sing or talk about some of the songs that they have heard. Talking may include an expression of the feelings which were created by the sounds of the music. Children may ask and answer questions or they may respond by just sitting quietly and thinking.

Expression through singing in a large group can also be meaningful if the songs selected are significant to the child and related to the unit of study. Songs used should always be true to Scripture. The melody needs to complement the words. It should be simple and within the vocal range of the children. The words need to deal with concrete ideas. Children think very literally and are unable to bring meaning to symbolism. The subject matter covered in the songs chosen for and by children needs to include variety. Songs may reinforce Bible truths, relate to modern life, encourage praise, or review a story sequence. Songs about other countries can be used to reinforce missionary activities. You will need to select a basic songbook which will meet your needs, and also use song suggestions that will be included in the curriculum materials.

TEACHING A NEW SONG

Use a variety of methods to teach new songs. Words may be written on a chart and illustrated by the children. Songs may be used in a rebus fashion, substituting simple drawings for some of the words. Words may be left out and supplied by children adding word cards and/or pictures in the appropriate places. Acting out a song in pantomime or with costume will help the learner make the meaning of the song a part of themselves. Simple stick puppets held up at the appropriate time permit the child to participate in a musical activity in a different way.

A new song needs to be presented in a way that will insure the child of a success experience. The following sequence will be helpful to the teacher who is uncertain as to how to present a new song.

1   Sing the song while the children listen. Use a piano, Autoharp, or other instrument. The melody notes may be played as the teacher sings.

2   Talk about the words. Pictures may be used to clarify meanings.

3   Sing the song again.

4   Sing the song with the children.

5   Sing the song by phrases. The teacher sings a

phrase, and asks the children to repeat the phrase. Then the group sings the whole song together.

6 Use the song for several sessions so that the children will become familiar with the words and the music. A variety of musical experiences may be planned for the same song.[1]

CHILDREN CAN CREATE MUSIC

As children participate in successful musical activities, they may want to create some music and words of their own. These will be related to the needs and feelings of the child. Children may be motivated to create their own songs in a variety of ways. Listening to music, looking at pictures or reading stories, poems, and Bible verses may all lead to the desire to write a song. Songs are written with greatest success with a small group of children. Upon completion, they may be recorded on a chart, illustrated and shared with the entire group. A song will emerge as children combine words and melody, as they try out the combination, and then make changes until the sound is pleasing to them. Occasionally, children will need to be given a pitch or starting place for the melody. The bells, zither or piano may be used to help play back the new tune as the children experiment with it. A song will naturally evolve as children are encouraged to work with music. If the activity is initiated by the teacher with comments such as "Let's write a song," or "Now is the time for us to write a song," children will probably feel inadequate and will not be ready for a song-writing experience. Follow the leadership of the learner and provide the subtle support and guidance that may be needed.

Children may need to work in intermediate stages before creating a complete song with both words and melody. The following sequence may be a helpful guide.

1 Add new words or verses to a known song.

2 Fill in a few new words to a familiar song, such as the one below:*

Tell me the story of____(Moses)____,

How he was____(brave)____.

*Words were written to the song "Tell Me the Stories of Jesus," No. 118, *Everyone Sings*.

Tell me the story of___(Joseph)___,
Sold as a___(slave)___.

Tell me of___(Jesus)___,
Friend of everyone.
Tell me a___(story)___.
Stories are___(fun)___.

Children may be helped to write words for a new song if they are given a list of words which may suggest ideas for a song.

3 Write words for a song. Base the simple verse on a Bible truth as it relates to you or let your song tell a Bible story.

4 Put a tune or melody with the words. Use an instrument to help work out the tune.

5 Practice singing and playing the song.

6 Be ready to teach it to the children who did not participate in the musical experience.

USING MUSICAL INSTRUMENTS

The use of instruments as a part of musical experiences in the children's department should be considered. If space in your classroom is at a premium, consider removing the piano and using a smaller instrument that can be used by the children. Several different instruments are available tò us for very nominal investments.

The *Autoharp* is a very popular, easy-to-use instrument. It is made up of a series of strings and chord bars. It is played when the selected chord bar is pushed and the instrument strummed. Most songbooks have Autoharp chord markings above the musical staff. In the beginning, children will be able to strum the Autoharp while the teacher presses the correct chord bar. Then two children may work together with one of them strumming while the other presses the chord bars. Finally, one child is able to put both actions together by pressing the chord bar and strumming the strings at the same time. Children may use the Autoharp during small group time, or the child may accompany the large group singing. In all cases, it will be important for the child to be able to play the song well before doing it with the total group.

A *zither* is another small instrument that may be used by the children independently in the music center, or to accompany the large group. The zither is a simple, one-octave, stringed instrument. A card cut to the shape of the zither is slipped in under the strings. The card is marked with a series of circles and dots to indicate the placement of notes on the zither. Words may be included on the card. The zither is played by the child as he plucks the string at the place where the dot or note is placed.

A set of *melody bells* will provide children the opportunity of playing a tune that may be sung by the small group or large group. Melody bells are manufactured in sets of eight, providing just one octave. Several children need to work in a cooperative group to play the bells. The song is marked with a colored paper circle or dot pasted on the chart with the words of the song. At least four children must work together, and the activity could include eight children very easily. Children can usually handle two bells at the same time, but if eight children are involved, each child may have one bell.

Tone bells are bells fastened to blocks of wood. They are played by striking the bell with a stick. One child is needed for each tone bell. In the beginning, the teacher will need to help the children select the bells that will be needed for a given song. Children strike their bell at a given signal from the teacher or child leader.

Think of the differences in the more traditional music program in the children's departments. Singing has usually been used by the large group in the worship program. The songs are selected by the teachers and there is little real participation on the part of the children. Let's accept the challenge of using music in a variety of ways. Let's capitalize on the child's interest and enthusiasm by providing ways of choice and participation in musical activities. The joyous sound of children singing and playing instruments is truly an experience of praise to God.

CHECK TASK—*Practice using some of the suggested instruments that are available to you. Prepare the music that can be used by children with the zither and/or Autoharp. Write a new song or new words for a familiar melody related to a Bible lesson that you will be teaching. Help children share the experience of writing a song.*

CHAPTER FOURTEEN

THERE'S STILL MORE . . .

OBJECTIVE—*to explore additional Bible learning activities that will provide flexibility and variety in the selection of activities for a group of children.*

When the responsibility of classifying ideas, thoughts and objects is completed, there are always a few items left that just don't fit neatly into established categories. This is the case with creative Bible learning activities. So read through these miscellaneous ideas and add some of your own to spice up that hour on Sunday morning.

Model Building: (1, 2, 3, 4, 5, 6; S) Children thoroughly enjoy model building. Many fourth, fifth and sixth graders are model enthusiasts. Let's grasp this interest and put it to work in our Bible learning activities. Children find it very difficult to visualize a marketplace, a synagogue, clothing and homes of Bible times, and items from other countries related to a missionary study. Children can and will combine research activities with model building, and as a result will have a more accurate picture and understanding of faraway times and places. Often, model building is not really creative. In an effort to reach an accurate conclusion, preplanned and prepared kits are put together, and the small group has only to read and follow precise and complete directions.

However, model building can have a measure of creativity and still maintain the accuracy that is needed for authenticity. Help the children to research the item that is to be built. List the materials needed to duplicate that item. Make a set of plans that will be precise enough to develop the item that is needed. Leave room for choice in matters of opinion, or in situations where there is an element of the unknown, even after the research is as complete as possible.

Models may be used as props for puppet plays, part of a diorama, or in displays and exhibits. A written explanation may accompany such displays, thus relating model building and written expression. Information will be shared and concepts strengthened as a result of this kind of experience.

Dioramas: (1, 2, 3, 4, 5, 6; S) The construction of dioramas may be an expression of the acquisition of information. A diorama may be built to illustrate a Bible story or a Bible verse. It may portray a modern day situation or be used in discussion for solving a problem. Usually the diorama is placed in a container about the size of a shoe box. A background scene is prepared from a painting, a crayon drawing, or a cut-and-paste activity. Figures are added to the diorama by being placed in front of the background. The dioramas may be shared with the total group, with another classroom, or may be used as a part of a display.

Maps: (3, 4, 5, 6; S and L) Children begin to look to maps for help in putting together events and places. Large, simple maps are needed for children's departments. Maps should be uncluttered, having only the most important geographical areas labeled. The overhead projector and map transparencies provide an opportunity for the total group to use maps at the same time. Maps will help children become acquainted with the places where Jesus lived. Children will be able to trace the journeys of Paul as well as better understand the distance involved in present-day missionary work. Map study has elements of research and language activity. An art activity may be included as children choose to make salt and flour or papier-mâché maps. World globes may be made with papier-mâché from a round balloon base.

Time Lines: (1, 2, 3, 4, 5, 6; S and L) Working with time lines will help children solve that very difficult concept of sequence in time. The events of the Bible become a confusing jumble if we are not careful. We sometimes jump from the birth of Jesus to Old Testament character studies and back to the New Testament again. Children need our help in putting events into the correct order. Time lines may be made on a large sheet of newsprint or butcher paper. Children may write the dates in order, and with each date, record significant events which occurred at that time. You may wish to fasten a string or cord across an unused portion of the room. Children may draw pictures or write sentences about a given period of time in the life of a Bible character. The pictures and statements may be fastened to the cord in the correct order. Spring clothespins will secure the pictures.

Service Projects: (1, 2, 3, 4, 5, 6; S and L) Children of all ages may feel the joy of giving, loving and helping as they plan simple projects that will be of assistance to other people. The aim of our service projects in which we involve ourselves and our classes should be to meet a real need. The child should enter into the project with no thought or reward for himself.

Missionary projects need to become an integral part of the life of the child. Children need help in becoming well acquainted with a missionary family and a mission field. Through research, interview and letter writing, determine the needs of the missionary. Some of them can no doubt be partially met by an interested children's department. A burning concern for missions begins in childhood.

Friends and neighbors, as well as family members, can provide daily opportunities for the child to be of service. Helping to finish the chores at home, being kind to a sick friend, working when you really want to play, are all possibilities for practical service. If there is a children's home or a home for the aged in your area, contact them to determine a number of projects that are suitable for children to complete.

Children have worked happily and diligently to collect clothing, food and toys for an Indian tribe. They have baked cookies for shut-ins. They have written letters and made get-well cards for people in hospitals or those who are ill at home. They have planned and presented a musical program at a home for elderly persons. They have sewn and stuffed stockings for children in the hospital at Christmas time. When planning projects for homes and hospitals, check with the administrators to be sure that your project is one that will be permitted and needed by the organization.

Bible Games: (1, 2, 3, 4, 5, 6; S) The use of Bible games is gaining increasing acceptance. Children like to play games. It is only natural for us to use their interest in an activity which, though they consider it play, will bring about many learning opportunities. Children are often not aware that the purpose of the game is to educate. Most games involve some social growth because the players interact during the game. Children learn valuable lessons in taking turns, fair play, consideration, and that very important lesson of following the rules.

Consideration of the element of competition in the game must be given very careful attention. The purpose of Bible learning games is not keen competition. In fact, some children react negatively to competition. Such a child would probably not choose the game center. Most games used at church have a few simple, well-defined rules. It is not necessary to be concerned with a complicated team organization. Each player plays without interference from the other players.

Recently, church leaders have expressed an increased interest in flexible and innovative materials. Games are really not so new. Commercially prepared Bible games have a place in the department. However, most curriculum materials suggest game ideas that can be easily made by the teachers. These games are directly related to the needs, interests, and abilities of the pupils, as well as to the curriculum.

Games can be designed that will give information, help develop correct attitudes and feelings, and review a certain portion of the unit plan. Look into your curriculum and construct some of the games that are suggested. Add some ideas of your own. Children will provide clues to the games that are needed by the group. As you observe and listen, you will be able to tell whether the available games are chosen by the children. You will be able to determine the kinds of games that the group would like to have. You may even have success in obtaining help from children or interested adults to create some of your own.

Children are truly fortunate when they are involved in an educational program with teachers who look ahead. They will have the opportunity to stretch and grow according to their individual needs, abilities and interests. The responsibility of teaching children is an awesome one. We cannot do an adequate job without the guidance and help of God. He has promised to be with us and to guide us. Surely, we can ask of Him, through prayer, a generous measure of patience and understanding which will help the children to become patient, understanding individuals. We can pray for wisdom and guidance as we study the Word of God in our preparation for teaching, so that children may gain the factual information from God's Word that they need. We can earnestly work to be sure that our lives are filled with the love of God for others. Children can be led to a loving, satisfying relationship with God because of their participation in a sound educational program based upon the Word of God and the needs of the learners.

CHECK TASK—*Prepare a card file or notebook system for your own use that will assist your children in the selection of appropriate Bible learning activities. If you choose to prepare a file, place a description of the activity together with a list of materials needed, hints for preparation of the work area, and helpful comments or evaluation of the activity on a card. Use one card for each activity. File them in categories used in this book, or add or change categories to meet your needs. Place new cards in the file as you discover new activities. Such a file will provide an accessible resource to aid in planning Bible learning experiences for the children with whom you work.*

FOOTNOTES

CHAPTER 8

1 · I Corinthians 3:9. From *The New English Bible, New Testament.* ©The Delegates of the Oxford University Press and the Syndics of the Cambridge University Press 1961, 1970. Reprinted by permission

2 · Matthew 22:21, *King James Version.*

3 · Elizabeth Allstrom. *You Can Teach Creatively.* (Nashville: Abingdon Press, 1970), p. 29.

4 · Jeremiah 33:3, *KJV.*

5 · I Thessalonians 2:8. *The Amplified Bible.* (Grand Rapids: Zondervan Publishing House, 1965.) Used by permission.

CHAPTER 9

1 · Phyllis Sapp. *Creative Teaching in the Church School.* (Nashville: Broadman Press, 1967), pp. 59-62.

CHAPTER 12

1 · Elsie Rives and Margaret Sharp. Adapted from *Guiding Children.* (Nashville: Convention Press, 1969), pp. 60-62.

2 · Rives and Sharp. *Guiding Children,* p. 63.

CHAPTER 13

1 · Rives and Sharp. *Guiding Children,* p. 170.

BIBLIOGRAPHY

Allstrom, Elizabeth. *Let's Play a Story.* New York Friendship Press, 1957

———, *You Can Teach Creatively.* Nashville: Abingdon Press, 1970.

Bigg, Morris L. *Learning Theories for Teachers.* New York: Harper & Row, 1964.

Bloom, Benjamin S. *Taxonomy of Educational Objectives in the Cognitive Domain.* New York: David McKay Co., Inc., 1965.

Bradford, Ann. *Working with Primaries through the Sunday School.* Nashville: Convention Press, 1961.

Chamberlain, Eugene and Fulbright, Robert G. *Children's Sunday School Work.* Nashville: Convention Press, 1969.

Cruickshank, Donald R. "What We Know About Learning," *The Instructor* Magazine. Darien, Conn.: June-July, 1966.

Curley, Lois. "Where Am I Going? And How Will I Know If I'm on the Way?" *TEACH.* Glendale, Calif: G/L Publications, Winter, 1970, p. 39.

Dinkmeyer, Don C. *Child Development, The Emerging Self.* Englewood Cliffs, N.J.: Prentice-Hall, 1965.

Hammond, Phyllis E. *What to Do and Why, Activities for Elementary Groups at Church.* Valley Forge: Judson Press, 1963.

Krathwohl, David R. *Taxonomy of Educational Objectives in the Affective Domain.* New York: David McKay Co., Inc., 1965.

Learning, Learning, Learning. (Pamphlet published by Ocean View School District) Huntington Beach, California, 1970.

Ministry Is for Children's Workers Too (Pamphlet published by the Sunday School Board of the Southern Baptist Convention). Nashville, Tennessee.

Law Nolte, Dorothy. "Children Learn What They Live." (The American Institute of Family Relations, 5287 Sunset Blvd., Los Angeles, California).

Richards, Lawrence O. *Creative Bible Teaching.* Chicago: Moody Press, 1970.

Rives, Elsie, and Sharp, Margaret. *Guiding Children.* Nashville: Convention Press, 1969.

Sapp, Phyllis. *Creative Teaching in the Church School.* Nashville: Broadman Press, 1967.

Smith, Charles T. *Ways to Plan and Organize Your Sunday School,* Children: Grades 1-6. Glendale, Calif.: G/L Publications, 1971.

Stith, Marjorie. *Understanding Children.* Nashville: Convention Press, 1967.

Taylor, Barbara J. *A Child Goes Forth.* Provo, Utah: Brigham Young University, 1964.

Theories of Learning and Instruction. 63rd Yearbook of the National Society for the Study of Education, University of Chicago Press, 1964.

𝒯rain for Effective Leadership

The impact of effective leadership can be felt in every area of your Sunday school. Train your leaders and teachers with **Success Handbooks** from ICL. Prepared by recognized authorities in Christian education, the handbooks in each series are especially designed for four basic age groups:
Early Childhood, Children, Youth, Adult.

Series 1, Ways to Help Them Learn

The Success Handbook on each level discusses the learning process, age characteristics, needs and abilities, plus proven teaching techniques.

Series 2, Ways to Plan and Organize Your Sunday School

The Success Handbook on each level offers guidance in building your Sunday school with a plan consistent and effective at every level.

Each Success Handbook $1.95.
set of all 8: $14.95.

Regal Books
Glendale, California